THE AGE OF ACTUALIZATION

A Handbook for Growing Elder Community

D1177001

Book and cover design by the authors;
front cover photographs by the authors and Batra Njana; back cover, Batra Njana

THE AGE OF ACTUALIZATION
A Handbook for Growing Elder Community

ISBN 978-1497595156

First printing May, 2014 in the U.S.A.

Gratitude is offered to Angeles Arrien for the practices found in her work
The Four-Fold Way: Walking the Paths of the Warrior, Teacher Healer, and Visionary
and to Coleman Barks for his translation of Rumi's "The Soul of Community"

Authors:
David "Lucky" Goff – dg1140@sonic.net
Alexandra Hart – ahart@sonic.net
Sebastopol, California

The Soul of Community

The soul of community
is coming through us,
light on its forehead,
old stories in its right hand,
unknowing freedom in its left.

Don't ruin this chance
with easy promises,
politeness,
pretenses of knowledge,
or elegant quotes.
The help that has been longed for is here.
Join with other great souls.

Gathering together becomes a ceremony,
approaching Mystery.

Meaning: pass quickly through your being
into absence, unknowing and emptiness.

The self of your name and fame
secures you
with a new knot
every moment.

Personal identity is a sheath
The unique one resides within.

Reality unites
worn covering,
with our mysterious,
unencumbered, nature.

Look closely.
In community,
Love is purifying love.

—Rumi re-translation by David "Lucky" Goff
via Coleman Barks)

TABLE OF CONTENTS

Using this Handbook

— *Alexandra*

Lucky and I have decided to each create mostly separate pieces for this Handbook, as our styles are distinct, just as our roles have been in putting together the Elders Salon which instigated all this. We believe that part of the success of our elders' project has been due to our differences. So, as you will see, we provide bylines. While we both have much experience with groups and with community-building activities, again we have come from very different points of view. This has been a source of growth for me, not least in the developmental move from "tolerating difference" to appreciating and welcoming differences that arise.

A minor area of difference is in our writing choices. In our elder groups we have been discouraging the use of "we/our" and "you," choosing to speak as much as possible in "I statements." This becomes very awkward when speaking about generalities. We have discovered that learning more and more about not accepting cultural attitudes is freeing, and that cultural attitudes are often spoken as "we." Sometimes using the pronouns "I" and "one," while avoiding the trap of speaking for someone else who may not at all agree with one, becomes just too cumbersome for me, distracting the flow of meaning. So I ask forbearance if I sometimes write generally, apparently including you in something with which you don't agree.

There is also a politically correct gender pronoun problem when trying to speak of what a person might feel when he or she (they?) is/are referred to ungrammatically. That sentence was constructed to demonstrate the difficulty, which you are all likely to have encountered. I may retreat to the accepted masculine reference (in English grammar), or alternately use something made-up like "s/he" or simply allow the ungrammatical to occur. Lucky is on his own here as well.

A larger difference in what we provide here is that I am prone to let you know the mechanics of what we have done to create the Elders Salon and he is more prone to tell you of the "inside job" and the more hidden discoveries we have encountered along the way. I am grateful to his skill in flushing out these characteristics and his competence in putting words to that part of the Salon experience.

I believe that for any group of elders (if not the "merely old") to find a community engaging, they will be happiest finding their own style. Still, it may be helpful to have a bit of early guidance toward getting the group into more substantive discussion while including a good deal of freedom. We found that most of us were wary at first that a group of this sort might simply not be our cup of tea — for myself, because I couldn't see myself as *old!* Later I came to appreciate my age and age cohorts with a sense of pride. To counter this wariness, a speedy entry into what truly engages our minds is of benefit. Practice saying one's age proudly is as well. Format and structure can, to some degree, aid in this process; therefore, I shall provide some of what we did. Do not interpret our path as prescriptive but rather as informational, with an intention to point a possible direction if it is useful.

Introduction

— *Lucky*

I had just finished writing *Embracing Life*. I thought I might die
before I got through it, but that didn't happen. During that writing I
developed a desire to work with older people. Being oriented to human
development I found myself speculating that the farthest reaches of
human development were more likely to occur amongst old people, the
most experienced of our kind. I wanted to find out if this was indeed
likely. Because I hadn't reached the end, and I am Lucky, I was moved by
my community into a new home. In the process I met Alexandra (who
hereafter I refer to as Xan).

She was trying to help the new residents of this development become
a community. I don't understand why, completely, but we became
friends enough that I was on the scene one day when she said she would
like to create an on-going group of old people. I think she was mainly
interested in inquiring into the unfinished business of the 60's and 70's.
I had the audacity (I didn't know her very well yet) to ask her if I could
do it with her. I think she surprised us both by saying "yes," even more
audaciously.

We didn't know it, but that moment turned out to be quite fortuitous.
From the first meeting of the Salon, which was composed mostly of her
friends, something unusual began to take place. Now nearly four years
later we are pausing and trying to capture some of what has happened in
this handbook. I have been surprised, delighted, humbled, heartened,
and greatly moved by the words, hands, and hearts of old folks. The
Elders Salon has transported me into a new world. In this place
discovering each other has amounted to discovering ourselves.

Xan and I have had the good fortune to provide a social space that
allowed the gifts of old people to become visible. Without really
knowing what we were doing we tapped into a kind of mother lode. Our
emphasis was upon consciousness raising because we quickly learned
that many old folks didn't even know what they were capable of, but
this emphasis was rapidly joined by community-building. Caring turns

out to be one strength of old folks, an attribute that took us deeper into each other's lives and brought connection. As people got to know each other and learned more about themselves, the Salon became an important bulwark against the ageist voices that seek to define old age for us. The Salon, this group of old people, began to develop its own voice and its own ideas about what aging is about. Old people defined for themselves what they were up to.

I don't know if this handbook will help anyone start an elder community. It is intended to be of help, but I have learned that old people have too little time and energy to waste on simply good ideas. It seems to me that old folks are hungry for real meaning. It is my hope that there is enough real meaning within these pages to feed some of that hunger. I don't kid myself, however; the real food lies in the connections made. Feed each other with yourselves. That is what lies at the heart of elder community; it is why it works for us; and it is a process by which old people discover the miracle of who they are.

HANDBOOK

for

Growing an Elder Community

Life doesn't care about what you know;
it only cares about who you are.

— *Anonymous*

It is not by muscle, speed or physical dexterity

that great things are achieved,

but by reflection, force of character and judgment;

in these qualities

old age is usually not only not poorer,

but it is even richer.

— *Cicero*

Prologue

— *Lucky*

Aging is a favor to us. All the losses, hardships and joys of growing older wise us up. As our bodies and memories become less reliable, something else is happening, turning us grey and ripe. This is what this handbook is all about: ripening, becoming actualized, living out life in the fullest manner. Aging not only greys and diminishes us; it alters our awareness and thoroughly changes the way we see life. While we are losing the life we once knew, we are gaining a new, riper one.

This handbook is designed to help us aging folks discover what a favor aging can be. Luckily, this handbook cannot do that alone. The favor that aging brings is most visible, most experiential, most palpable in a community of older people. Interestingly enough, the benefits of aging become clearest within, when one is connected to others.

This is a time of deep actualization and freedom. What has been only a wild and desperate hope, now is coming to fruition. One of the favors of aging is that Life has honed one down, making time and energy (called retirement) for the uniqueness within. Coming to the surface now is something of each soul's truest nature, and it becomes richer when shared with others having similar experiences. This is the time in life when one can be culturally dismissed, and it is the time when one can be alone enough to finally be oneself. While one's truest nature is being brought to the fore, community with others is useful. A compelling social experience brings friends, recognition, and renewed meaning.

Meaning and connection are the goals of this handbook. Aging sets us up, but ripening is up to us. Happiness is related to fulfillment. Becoming fully oneself, being rich internally, goes a long way but isn't enough. What's called for is the opportunity to participate, to share life experiences, to discover unknown meaning together, to care about and be cared about, to face the future as part of a larger whole. This provides the ultimate nurturance for what is coming forward. It is as if Life has provided the best place for fruiting to occur. And that place is within ourselves and within community.

People discover themselves, each other, and what is possible in community. Old people who, by and large, are ignored in the social reality of our culture discover themselves, the true value of their attributes, their ability to connect, what they have to give, the perspective they hold, and the vision that sets them free in a community of age-cohorts. Frequently, old people don't tend to know what they are made of until they start connecting with other old people. Then something more fully enlivening happens; the true gifts of aging become clear. This handbook is dedicated to nurturing that possibility.

Community-building is an art form, not a science. There is no guarantee that a group of strangers will experience community. In this culture at this time obstacles to community exist. Yet, it is just those difficulties, plus the emerging capabilities of the old, that make coming together such a surprising gift. Caring is what is left to the old. It is what we are good at, and it is what ties us all together. This handbook gives that caring a chance.

Basic Philosophy

— *Lucky*

Life is the teacher. Each of us is endowed with the basic freedom of knowing for ourselves the way towards our own uniqueness. Becoming ourselves is an inside job. Others may help along the way, but the ultimate unfolding is unique, like no one else, and is utterly idiosyncratic. Life guides each of us home, to ourselves. The recommendations of others, no matter how well intended, are based upon their own experiences, which may be authentic, even profound; but each of us is uniquely guided by Life into our most original and authentic form. Life is the guide.

Self is our gift. The most incredible and beautiful gift each of us possesses is our own self, the gift that Life has endowed us with. The truest benefit we can provide to others is to be true to ourselves. By being present and by being true, an alternative to all posturing is presented. Self-possession is seen as a real possibility, and Life's diversity is affirmed. The greatest gift of old age is the actualization of Life's capacity in each of our lives. Self is our actualization of Life, and it is the greatest gift we have to give.

Community is the ripening ground, the practice field, where access to the gift of self most meaningfully unfolds. Life can unfold the self, and does, without community; but community is the place where the gift of self is most meaningfully given and where recognition occurs. Human community, because it is a smaller form of the much larger web, most palpably provides a sense of connection with others and the larger Cosmos.

The irritating complexity of social diversity, which appears in genuine community, provides the honing friction that is necessary for the development of complex and nuanced selves. By weathering the complex challenges of community, one proves oneself and simultaneously reveals the self as a gift of Life for all to share and relish. Community provides the place that can naturally hold and nurture this kind of development. Immersion in others coaxes out of each of us our greatest uniqueness and makes explicit our beauty. This empowers individual and community alike, making collaboration practicable. This is how the gift of Life grows.

Hosts

— *Lucky*

Doing something as unusual as starting and hosting an elders'
community is an on-going act of service. Like any act of service it is
bound to educate all those involved. The process of growing is a humble
one. Each increase in consciousness is accompanied by a realization
that one has failed to be judicious and inclusive in the past. To set out
with the objective of growing a community means that one must be
willing to forgive oneself. In essence a community grows itself. This is an
essential attribute for doing real service, helping the group find its own
will. Forgiveness is especially recommended for the hosts, as forgiveness
takes a while to take hold in the group-at-large.

Hosting and guiding a burgeoning elders' community requires no
specialized skills. That means that hosts do not need to be therapists,
community experts, social activists, or politically astute. In fact, all of
these forms of knowledge might be troublesome. Essentially, hosts need
only be as human as possible; this means letting one's vulnerability,
passion, and willingness to learn out loud (and in the moment) show.
The larger the desire to learn is in the hosts, their willingness to be fully
befuddled about growing older, the greater the likelihood of touching
the same place in other elders. Remember, the greatest gift the hosts
have to give is their own being.

Hosting and guiding the growth of an elder community is a balancing
act. A community must grow of its own accord. No amount of good
guidance assures this. The willingness to risk publicly impacts the group
and catalyzes deepening intimacy. Listen for these moments, and affirm
how they grow trust, meaning, and connection. You and your hosting
team are not responsible for making such moments happen, but you
can be open to them happening and encourage them, both within the
group, and within yourselves.

Caring, for humans, is deeply ambivalent. So is community with others.
There is a level of vulnerability that comes with each. While this is to
be encouraged, and old people often have more capacity for it, real

communal intimacy is the exception not the rule, and must evolve in its own time. Patience, listening, and caring enough to let intimacy evolve are all skills innate to elders, which will only show up over time. The best thing a host or host team can do is surrender attachment to having anything happen at all. Elders' community is a natural phenomenon that simply needs a chance to happen. If you and your team can be enough in front *and* get yourselves out of the way, then you've done all you can to optimize that chance.

Evolving our Host Team

— Alexandra

The initial impulse may come from one or two people or be quickly passed among more. Our experience tells us that at least two, ideally a man and a woman with differing attitudes and skills which will mean that if you satisfy *both* of you, you'll satisfy more of a larger group. We could have used a larger core hosting group from earlier on, simply because it creates a wider knowledge, listening, and feedback base — more creativity. It can also slow down the process in the beginning because so many decisions have to be made. Group decisions are always slower in the making, though often speak better to more people since they represent a wider range.

When we, after four years, invited a few people who were core to the continuing salon to serve as a Guidance Council, we also announced to our whole group that we were doing so and invited anyone who had thoughts and ideas about the ongoing nature of the group activities to come as well. We ended up with six more people. Coming in later, they didn't fear that they would be saddled with more responsibility than they were ready for, as they were already well on-board.

This Council has been very helpful as the responsibility for creating each new event was spread over eight people instead of two. This also began to grow a sense of ownership or co-leadership as these folks felt capable of taking on at least one salon or more on their own or in pairs. We also get feedback about what works and doesn't work so well for various people and we get a break on the burnout front.

Getting Started

— Alexandra

Assuming you've decided to try establishing an Elders Salon, you've met with whoever is cohosting, and you're ready to start. I'll give some suggestions from our experience about place, time, who and how to invite people, and agendas.

Place

What our Transition Sebastopol has yearned for is a clubhouse, but we've really never been able to manifest one. What we have for our Elders Salon is a cohousing common house where Lucky lives and which blessedly comes free for our use because of this. Finding a place where you don't have to charge to cover rent is ideal. We believe it is one of the major reasons we have been able to create a community of people who are on an equal basis with no concern for status or class. (See "Free and Freedom", p. 40, by Lucky.) Be creative in a search for a regular, free venue. Because services for senior citizens strikes a cord in many hearts, you may find a church or organization that is willing to make a space available to you.

Because we settled into a cohousing common house we had a kitchen available and a big hot water dispenser, cups and saucers, and refrigeration. This made it easy to always have hot tea and filtered water available, but means there's always a little cleanup.

Time

If you want the older folks (from their late 70's on) to come out, it needs to be early enough to get them home relatively early. If you want the folks who are pre-retirement (Baby Boomer age), then you'll need to start after work hours with time for a meal. This doesn't leave much leeway unless you can set it up for Saturday or Sunday daytime hours. Many of the older group won't like driving after dark, either, so our solution of 4th Thursday of the month (3rd Thursday in November and December because of holidays) cuts out a few of our people in the early dark days of winter. We start at 6:30 p.m. and end at 8:30 so folks can be home by 9:00. We also have an informal gathering on Friday afternoons from 3:30 to 6:00 (closing time) at a local coffee house.

Getting out the Word

Ideally your group is connected to an entity with an email announcement list which you can use. Also, each one on your host team is likely to have friends in the community to enlist, especially for the first meeting. Perhaps there is a community email bulletin board or events announcement list you can use. Relying on print invitations is a difficult and ultimately unsustainable way to go. For the non-computing population you can rely on word of mouth and personal invitation for the first one, then make an inquiry about need and make a buddy system for those few who cannot receive emails.

After the first time or two you're likely to have a lot of people who were supporting the host team members dropping out and have the others making direct invitations to their friends. In this way those who are really into it begin to accrue. We have had between 20 and 40 people come to almost every salon we've had over the past 5 years, always with a few new folks, a certain number coming now and then, and a reliable core group.

It's very helpful to have one team member who is willing to keep up the mailing list and make up and send out the announcements on a regular basis. We use a Google Group list serve within the Transition Sebastopol main announcement system for Elders Salon announcements and another Elders Discussion list that any member can post to. Our membership consists only of being on the list or showing up at meetings. Our main hosting entity makes a calendar twice monthly that we appear on, and we regularly have about four events on every one issued. We also send a "designed" pasted-in email announcement at the beginning of the month and again a day or two ahead to remind folks.

Devising an Agenda

The first time we thought of all the things we thought older folks might want to have general information and conversation about. We didn't know whether they would want to have a person from outside representing Medicare or other health or social services say something and ask questions, talk about death and dying *(á la* a Death Café), just socialize, talk Transition topics, or really have a Wisdom Council or circle. So, we put lists on the walls in categories on pieces of newsprint and at some point gave colored sticky dots, maybe one red for top priority and four yellow to indicate interest. This was our agenda.

6:30   Arrive; Tea & Cookies
        Assess numbers and seating – potential topics sheets hanging on walls

6:40   Open with welcome, thanks to (host place), where things are Transition and what it is:
        "Transition Sebastopol serves to build a positive future by cultivating community resilience and responding to the great challenges of our times with inspired local action."

        What the Elder branch of Transition is in relation to the Salon and our interest in identifying what resilience means for Sebastopol elders

        Email list: pass around sheet and explain how it works (they can sign up for other Transition groups as well)

        General shape of evening and intention for future

        Reminder to SPEAK UP as many older people need volume

        Intros of the hosting folks

6:55   Introduce yourselves (This is [previous person] – and I am [name]. I'm [age].)

7:00   Overview of topics and using colored dots to choose top interests

7:10   Set up a fish bowl: What are your top concerns for the future of Sebastopol elders and which topics do you want to see us bring up for consideration?

7:45   Gather into loose groups of 5 or 6 to further explore common interests

8:10   Come back into large circle for Wisdom sharing

8:25   Close and apply dots, mill and talk

8:30 – 9:00   Clean up

Topics and Format

The primary interests settled into what I would call the developmental tasks of becoming an elder. In essence, the transition into elderhood is occurring for our generation at the same time change is also a major, ongoing fact in the larger world. A variety of transitions seem to be much needed at this time on the planet. Many of us came into the Salon environment rather wondering how we fit into all this change.

Truthfully, designing any meeting, format, or agenda should be primarily focused toward how to best enhance discovery of the elder experience and of one's dual position as a fully developing individual and a part of the developing community social group.

It didn't take long to discover that people at this stage of life *need* to talk to each other, compare experiences and notes, and discover how they can make the internal shifts that their bodies and life situations call for in order to live fulfilling, meaningful, and useful lives. Nor did it take long to discover that the quality of elder thinking and our capacity is different from how it was at younger ages. So the interaction with others helps a great deal in determining what "right action" looks like at this stage. Of course that's individual, though some of Lucky's writings in this handbook explore our some of our more general discoveries.

There is a list of some of our past topics and sample agendas in the "Deeper In" section, p. 71, but here's what we've settled into as a general form. Since one of the things many of us seem to be hungry for can be addressed by being witnessed and recognized, we try to create experiences and present topics (often posed as a question) that draw out authenticity and the opportunity to witness one another while hearing oneself. There are always a few new people, so making sure a brief, introductory round is made helps the group to arrive and settle. With only two hours, it's good to get to the heart fairly quickly, but everyone wants to get to know who the others are as well.

Introductions are important because people want to be able to remember names which makes some repetition useful, especially if you have new people joining the group as we usually do. A simple fact that a person can provide as they give their name can help. Sometimes providing one's age is a good choice because it can seem like everyone is older than oneself until you get used to your own location in the age range present. It also begins a process of undermining ageism, especially internalized ageism, which is itself an interesting topic. You have to be careful with asking a question that could stimulate a whole story unless you don't mind having the first round take up much of the available time. There are standard name-giving games that can be used, such as having each person sing their name followed by the group singing it back to them or having the second person repeat the first person's name then give their own, as in the first agenda that was provided above. I prefer something that is more personal that can add to my knowledge of each person.

We let people mill and settle for a few minutes, then start with a welcome, give basic space and procedural info, any housekeeping, and announcements. The general topic is presented, then we elicit the group response to the topic in whatever format seems to be best suited (go-rounds in the large circle, small groups, fishbowl, something more experiential, or combinations of these). Some people prefer the large circle; others speak more easily in a dyad or small group, so we try to mix it up from one month to the next. If there has been a small group to draw out specific responses, then we will return to full group for a sense of the highlights, and it is in this last 30 or 45 minutes that surprising wisdom is likely to coalesce. Sometimes it is hard to stop to close, though keeping to the promised time frame is important. One of our members is a poet and our closing has come to be his sharing a poem that seems to relate to our evening's experience. Cleanup and mixing a little more occur as people gather themselves up to go home.

One facilitation style mentioned above that may need more description is "fish bowls" since there are differing ways of facilitating them. I suggest keeping it simple so that either as many people as are interested in speaking to a subject go to the center, with the others witnessing from the outside of the circle, or a specified number of chairs are set up (say five) and once a person has said all he or she wants to say, s/he leaves the circle and another person from the outside circle can fill that space.

If the topic is gender-specific, it could be one gender in the center then reverse to the other. Then within that circle people can be directed to interact with cross-talk as desired or to speak one at a time, staying as long as they like.

Gathering

— Lucky

Something magical happens when a group of old people come together. Of course there are all of the standard kinds of social anxiety about what might happen; but there is something else, a sudden recognition that other older people have an interest in what being older means. What's possible? To find out requires starting someplace.

The task of the hosting team is two-fold: create a congenial space and help the meeting be as compelling as possible. The first matter involves simple common sense. Make sure the space is congenial for a group of old folks. Make sure to explicitly ask the group if there are any special needs that require attention. This can help the group find comfort with hearing loss, sight impairment, chemical sensitivity, and any other disabilities. If there is going to be a break, then that should be made clear, and when should be identified. If people are expected to take care of themselves (my recommendation), then that should be made explicit. The time-frame of this meeting and all meetings should be clearly stated and kept.

The making of a compelling meeting is more challenging. It is true that one can lead a horse to water, but one cannot make the horse drink. So it is with a group of older folks. Initially, the hosting team must take a major portion of the responsibility for presenting a plausible way for people to get acquainted and to get into something of concern to old folks. Later, the group will have ways of indicating what is of interest.

Here, it is important that the hosting team use itself well. This theme will be reiterated throughout. The hosting team has created for itself an enormous learning opportunity. Listen, try to stay present, and check out your assumptions with the group. The diverse reactions of the host team will mirror those of the group. Everyone on the team should be taking the pulse of the group and sharing these perceptions and assumptions with each other in your organizational meetings. Where the group goes will be, to some degree, aided by the readings of the hosting team.

If the goal is to create community within the circle of older folks, then community must be the focus of the hosting team. How each of you holds the other members of your team and what you learn about yourselves and each other as you interact will likely parallel the learning in the larger group. The emergence of communal feelings in the group will happen as those same feelings emerge within the hosting team. Older folks have been shown to have a greater capacity for relating well, if given the chance. As the hosting team discovers these capacities within themselves, they are much more likely to notice and invite out those same capacities in the larger group.

No facilitation team lasts long and truly serves its constituency if it is unable to cope with surrendering control. It is as important to be able to surrender an agenda as it is to create one. So, the practice of surrendering outcome is essential. The emergence of communal feelings in the group must be the group's own authentic natural expression, not the host team's. To serve well, hosts must merge into the group and let go of personal concerns in order to further group concerns.

Remember, Life is the teacher, the chief motivator, the great organizer, the deep, and the tie that binds. It is part of humans' natural inheritance to be social animals, to crave meaningful interaction. Some would say we humans are endowed with the instincts of curiosity, play, and sociability. The hosting team merely has to find a good starting place, then the group will take over. If the host team can join in and not get in the way, then it is likely that something will happen. Let yourselves be moved by what is happening; share yourselves. The process benefits when anyone really shows up authentically.

For community to grow is not so different from how any of us grow. There will be moments where there will be some discomfort. This is natural. Groups have to learn how to deal with it. It is customary in our culture to avoid social discomfort, but learning and bonding depend upon the group's capacity to go beyond social norms. The hosting team can convey trust in such developments by predicting them and by meeting these moments with curiosity. The hosting team models, as best it can, the social traits that will lead toward greater connection.

Connecting emotionally is, amongst us humans, an ambivalent thing. This is very human and natural; we want to be known and fear the same thing. We want to connect, but fear what connection will deliver or ask of us. Opening our hearts almost always means opening through hurt, rejection, and disappointment. True community takes time and has multiple levels. Let it unfold, and let yourselves and the group approach it slowly. Caring is the currency that will make all of this work. Old people know more about caring than most. They simply need some encouragement. That is a gift that becomes available when old people gather.

Finally, a natural part of the ambivalence that people feel is based upon the sure knowledge that community, real social connection, will ask each of us to grow ourselves.

Not just in the ways we want, or are good at — so compassion is called for. The hosting team is likely to feel this need first. What is done with it may well set the tone for the group. This is one of the valuable learning opportunities that the hosting team has set up for itself: developing compassion for self, others, and this precious world we live in. Community emerges along with compassion and caring.

Interactions

— *Lucky*

In essence the hosting team has responsibility for making an event that tries to balance content with process, guidelines with freedom, fun with seriousness, and consciousness-raising with community-building. Essentially, this impossible task can only be approximated, and then with a lot of help and good will from the participants. Close is good enough, if the group feels that you have their interests in mind. Have fun, enquire into topics and group processes, and remind everyone this is an experiment in growing an elder community.

Start somewhere compelling enough to draw curiosity. Meetings will evolve. Through paying attention (one of the Four-fold Way guidelines) the hosting team will come to notice many things about the group that will help it fulfill its role. All one has to do is learn to set the original conditions and then track the group. You will notice that this handbook offers few examples because groups always have their own idiosyncratic nature, especially, a group of old folks (see Facilitation of Elder Groups, p. 68). Initially, the team provides a beginning place then moves on to paying close attention to what is going on within the group.

So, what is meant by "setting the original conditions?" This entails affirming the consciousness-raising and community-building goals of the event and describing some of the means for getting there. For instance, one will want to introduce the hosting team, ask for patience and cooperation, describe the ways of interacting, affirm the guidelines (show up, pay attention, tell the truth, and surrender attachment to outcome are the ones we like), and ask for permission to proceed. The confidence and togetherness of the hosting team will help buffer any natural social anxiety in the group. The group will test everything the host team says to find out if it is real. This might happen from the get-go, but should be expected at some time. Eventually, the hosting team will arrive, with the help of the group, at a standard way to open and close each meeting.

It is good for the hosting team to introduce content and processes. This promotes learning and social engagement. Meaning and connection are the key elements, which will make this endeavor compelling. Track the quality of engagement you perceive in the room. Craft the events so as to increase the level and significance of contact and interaction. Good conversation — questions about meaningful topics, and stimulating peers — are all sorely missing from old people's lives. Besides that, old folks cannot discover the value of what they hold for the larger community until they begin to know each other (and themselves).

It is always good to have questions. My partner in hosting says, "a good question is extremely valuable." She's right. A good question can facilitate a deep discussion, evoke connection, and raise consciousness. Look for questions that directly relate to the process of growing older in this era. Old people are so subject to unquestioned stereotypes. So, questioning is a pathway to freedom from the cultural trance. It is a very good way of throwing off the invisibility cloak that haunts old folks. Begin with questions, and watch for their emergence. They tend to take a group into the depths.

The hosting team will be under the group's scrutiny. The team, like it or not, is going to serve as a model of what is possible. This is good for the burgeoning community and for the learning of the host team, too. Remember, there is a parallel process between the host team and the larger group. This can be relied upon to increase understanding and development of each. Hosting is a great learning privilege.

We recommend the use of some minimal guidelines. This can be tricky. Older people are highly sensitive to the level of freedom around. They want to know if they are free to express and discover themselves in the circle. Unfolding and experimentation with self are what this whole process is about. So, guidelines that are useful to increase focus and social cohesion must be held carefully. They are useful as guides, but not as rules. Our recommendation is to encourage play and the creative use of the guidelines, while holding firmly to how they can help increase the quality of information and value of social sharing.

For very similar reasons cross-talk is not encouraged. The goal of our work together is to build a place where all forms of belief have an opportunity for expression. It is not to fix, heal, or convert anyone. All flags (beliefs) are welcome, but to preserve the chances for community, none should prevail. Proselytizing is also not encouraged. These assertions of the supremacy of belief will happen very naturally at first. But with appropriate guidance from the hosting team this pattern of interaction will slowly disappear. Eliminating this tendency gently removes old patterns of dominance and provides, instead, a more egalitarian and learning-full social space.

The tendency your team is most likely to see is a tendency to talk about things, not feelings. Our goal has been to foster caring. Toward this end the hosting team tries to create a space that is congenial to feelings. Caring is a feeling. It strengthens and grows when the feeling dimensions of our shared experience are expressed. Encourage the showing of feelings, more than talking about them. Feelings break the heart open, and this is the fountainhead of caring.

Lastly, as much as possible, cultivate an attitude of play. What is happening is fun (old folks' fun). It offers chances for humor and creativity. Modulate fun with learning and connection. Use group enjoyment as the guide. This is a Goldilocks sort of thing — the team is looking for the "just right" balance. Go for it! Death is bearing down on all of us, so live it up a little in each other's presence. Learn together the potentials held by aging!

More on Interacting

— Alexandra

The most important thing we've done, I believe, is to provide a congenial setting where older folks with a Transition/sustainability-conscious outlook can interact meaningfully. These people (we) are also in transition within themselves due to encountering an entirely new landscape in the aging process from other generations of aging folks. We've never been at this stage of life before, either. Having a place to explore what it actually is like for others and what it reveals to us about ourselves aids in the discovery of how to hold our own aging process. It also helps to separate inherited and projected cultural attitudes toward being old from our own personal experience and what we each can make of the journey, freeing us further.

And, as Lucky points out above, getting to the fun part of knowing people, revealing who one really is and being received without judgment, generates such caring and community feeling. This seems so much easier at this stage of life now that I have a capacity to be fairly nonreactive with people who are very different from myself, and that who we've each been in our younger days is more or less irrelevant.

As for guidelines, don't use them like a cop. Setting them originally and having them listed on the wall to be referred to only at need, is my suggestion. Cross-talk can be fine in dyads and small groups but can disrupt communications in a larger group. We have found that some people like the more intimate 2-5 person group size because they feel more comfortable speaking — and everyone gets more opportunity to speak. Others really like the large group conversations because the group wisdom has more points of view to emerge from. Mix it up!

Consciousness-Raising

— Lucky

What makes elder community so vital to a lot of old people is the chance to explore out loud the process of aging. Old people have a hunger for meaning. This really became clear to us early on. Our Elders Salon is (and elder community can be) a place devoted to community-building and consciousness-raising.

Living in an ageist culture it is not surprising how little is really known about aging. There is a dearth of truly useful information and a wealth of misinformation. Old people suffer under the weight of stereotypes and labor under culturally-induced, internalized ideas of what is possible in old age. The gifts the old have to give are unknown primarily because of cultural assumptions. Beliefs make the old invisible and rob old people of their self-esteem. In some ways one of the primary objectives of the salon (elder community) has become this kind of empowerment, helping us old people see the lies and opportunities that come with age.

The hunger for meaning that comes with aging isn't just a need to become better informed. Knowing more helps people become freer, but experiencing the wisdom of aging is another thing; it frees one to become oneself. Elder community unleashes people. It does so by inviting everyone to share their own perspective on a host of things that matter in making of one's latter years into a life worth living. Meaning isn't really about becoming better informed. Real meaning emanates from the best uses of information. Seeing and hearing how others are struggling with the issues of age provide perspective and resilience. Connecting people leads to sharing, and that raises general awareness.

Meaning is enriched by interaction. Take for example the statement, "Death happens to us all." On the surface that is a very meaningful assertion. Besides being intrinsically true, this statement is aided by being laden with implication. In a community the statement gains meaning by virtue of all the ways it can be taken. Death comes to everyone, but everyone doesn't deal with it in the same way. The fact that death touches us all is made more meaningful by the additional fact that it affects each of us differently.

The assertion that death is inevitable is meaningful but only thinly nutritious. Compare this to placing that same piece of information in an interactive environment. The fact of death and other explorations or events in a community context are more richly meaningful, thickly nutritious, and connective. The hunger for meaning that so many old people feel is fed better, in more life enhancing ways, by being shared.

Elder community has a catalytic effect. It takes what already has meaning and expands it. In this way old people are not only fed, but also nourished. They have a chance to experience additional meaning that comes through shared and creative responses to things. This enhances perspective, choice, meaning, and freedom. These are the attributes of raised consciousness, and they are the products of shared meaning. Old people are better at this than they used to be, and they benefit when they discover this fact.

Community-Building

— Lucky

Community is a complex phenomenon. A lifetime can easily be devoted to knowing its many permutations. A common mistake in community-building is the assumption that to build community one must know something about it. This is only partially true. It is helpful to know the feeling that arises as connections are made and become more vital (such a feeling is distinct). But many folks have been tripped up because they relied too heavily upon what they believed they knew about community.

Life doesn't care what you know; it only cares about who you are. This is the real core of community building — showing up. It is easier to relate to someone who is willing to let themselves be seen than it is to connect with someone who thinks they know something. So, instead of focusing upon the many attributes of community (see the "Deeper In" section for a thorough description of community), this handbook is emphasizing the aspects of being human that are most likely to engender emotional bonds. Community building is, therefore, not about information; it is about presence.

There are elements of personal presence that contribute to meaningful connections with others. These elements (which are described below) generate a social environment that is rare, magnetically inviting, and incredibly lively. People, when they are exposed to each other in this way, discover themselves, each other, and the mystery that binds them together. A feeling of caring arises from exposure — revealing the real heroism involved in being human. Feelings of connection extend out to include the world (the Transition component) *as* those who are present assume their full human stature.

These vital elements that create a congenial and magnetic environment are: presence, openness, learning, and reverence. Each of them is a personal practice that, when integrated and shared, generates a field that is highly magnetic and draws out similar qualities from others. As you will see, community-building depends upon revelation, and revelation depends upon practices that grow one's experience of self. The greatest gift you have to give your community, the penultimate contribution you can make to community-building, is to share yourself, to learn out loud, to make your uncertain journey a public passage. Then the rigors and beauty of being an aging human are evident to all. This mobilizes the heart, reassures the soul, and empowers everyone to be all they can be.

Presence

Showing up. This is what the Salon is all about. If old people can be themselves wherever they are, then the social world of our kind will mature. Elder community is desirable, and available as a practice field, a place to learn how to show up. It is also a very satisfying place to discover that showing up can be so meaningful, contributive, and bonding. Bring yourself to the dance; give what you've worked a lifetime to become. You are enough.

Openness

At the bottom of our existence there lives uncertainty. This is a common ingredient of being human, yet it is hard to live with. When folks allow themselves and each other to be uncertain publicly, then a whole new set of human possibilities comes into sight. Mature community is built around emptiness, the foregoing of knowing. One of our recommended guidelines is "surrender attachment to outcome." Practice openness, not knowing, for the benefit of connection with what is and for the benefit of gaining access to diverse elder experiences.

Learning

Reality is a complex, unknowable wonder. Sharing in the adventure of discovering the marvels contained within it has a stunning effect upon people. All are equal before mystery. Sharing a deep inquiry into the mystery of existence as it has come into being through each person present opens up a whole field of collective awareness. Learning together gives the old person a stimulating new take on Life, growing older, community, and other humans. Innocence is reborn.

Reverence

There is a larger being, some call it "Higher Power" or "Mystery." Staying humble, facing reality, and inquiring into what unfolds each of us is a deeply meaningful way to share with each other. A group of old people becomes an elder community when they do so. Keeping "something larger" ever at the center of group activities preserves and honors the glue that holds it all together. Cultivating this awareness is an elder necessity. Growing older educates us and makes the world a miracle worth sharing, as we become the product Life intended us to be.

In the final analysis growing an elder community is a shared endeavor. No one person can ever hope to do it alone. It is the by-product of a lot of people's caring. All one can do to promote what comes in the form of grace is be as real as possible. Fortunately, realness is an attribute that matures with aging. When old people come together, this attribute is already present. All that is needed is for mutual discovery to begin.

Essentializing

— *Alexandra*

There comes a time in everyone's aging process when you find you can no longer keep up your familiar pace (if you're lucky enough to survive into your older years). For women, if it hasn't happened previous to menopause, that particular life and body change is sure to start this up. Women are familiar with big changes in their hormones at various times in life, which brings a certain edge of recognition. Something's happenin' here, but you don't quite know what it is. Men, I can only guess, but they tend to wrinkle a little later and don't have the more dramatic body changes that help women come to terms.

In any case, while the timing is individual, aging will cause one to take stock. Necessity causes a process of sifting through one's use of time and energy. Sometimes a kind of "bucket list" starts to form. In our Elders Salon we began to call the sifting "essentializing" because you simply can't fit in as much in a day or an hour, and the sands of one's life are dribbling slowly away. You feel like you'd better make your choices count. Getting down to essentials: discarding the more frivolous activities, household items that suddenly seem in the way, relationships that don't seem appropriate or productive, concerns that you find you've outgrown — this kind of essentializing leaves you with more time for activities that you care about, that have more meaning, and that feed you. Eldering toward wisdom can begin to set in.

Reduction and Nutrition

It is also inevitable that this surrender of ways one has been in the past can feel like a reduction rather than a boon. The losses become more numerous. Loved ones have died; Life has weathered and scarred us; our bodies ache and we forget names. Yikes! But we are survivors! You don't get here without challenges and pain. Yet, here we are! We have survived! Some celebration, some gratitude, some awe about the journey can begin to creep in and the connection between grief and praise can dawn.

It is somewhere in this realm that our elders began to see "reduction" in a new light. Yes, we are reduced. It comes in many ways, both from inside or outside. My husband died, resulting in a loss of my home due to the mortgage crisis a few years ago and a loss of community in that we were living in cohousing. Everything went upside down. I even broke my right arm, followed by surgeries on both hands, which put a big kink in an existing art career I had been imagining I'd follow full-time.

A good cook knows a reduction in the production of much tasty food as a similar process to this elder phenomenon. There's less of it but it is richer and more flavorful. It can be quite extraordinary, in fact. After that loss I was freed to more easily become myself and follow my own new inclinations in surprising ways, living more simply with little excess. The reduction made me take more care with all my choices, paring down relationships and pastimes. I soon began work to create the Elders Salon, enlisting Lucky as a cohort.

Like the wisdom growing inside, all this richness began to feed me, nourish me, and lead me into new areas of my own growth and understanding of what I could and wanted to contribute. I began to feel a kinship with the folks who came to the salon, reducing the distance and learning from the shared wisdom that we discovered together. The aggregate expression of others in our exploratory discussions was truly feeding me! More meaning was coming my way through the individual experiences that were shared.

I am not alone. Many of those who continue to connect in this way, as elders, notice similar effects. Sitting together as we offer deeper observations, personal discoveries and stories to the circle, a palpable buzz or energy often emerges. I would describe my sensation as a receiving of nourishment I hadn't known I needed. I am being filled with some very necessary, unidentifiable kind of energetic food. We are caring about and for one another, becoming more resilient in the process. And many of us have found deeper self-acceptance and respect through our experiences and connections.

Dispensability

More recently, when Nelson Mandela died, I discovered a new elder capacity that is related but different from the reduction above, though it follows on its heels. In an interview when Mandela was deciding to leave public life, he said that his decision was partly due to knowing that he was dispensable. The reporter demurred, trying to dissuade Mandela from his point. But, no. Nelson knew that it is important to make way for younger people and that to follow one's path into the farther reaches of elderhood means knowing when to surrender to new energy. It is also likely to coincide with one's own need to go further within, slowly losing attachment to worldly pursuits.

As we journey toward the far end of life we must each grapple in our own way with the knowledge of mortality. I like to think of a metaphor of life processes as akin to sprouting, maturing, blossoming, fruiting, ripening, then finally, making seed. I have reached a stage of engaging with seed making, wondering what ways I and my generation will find to become viable seed. I wonder what such seed may contain for me as I lessen my attachments to experiencing life in familiar ways. I suspect I am making way for the Mystery.

Recognition

— Lucky

Old people respond to being seen. One of the hardest parts of getting old in this culture has to do with the loss of status. There is an invisibility cloak that seems to blanket the wrinkled and grey, rendering people to the periphery where they are unseen, devalued and demeaned. This is one important aspect of ageism. It hurts individuals, especially grey ones, and society alike.

Elder community provides a kind of antidote to the disabling force of invisibility. When old people see each other, they not only validate others but value themselves. This has a great salving effect. But, there is more possibility. Alexandra and I have found that old people thrive and often come more fully to life when they are actively admired, acknowledged, or recognized. There is a particular value in each of our lives. Admiration makes that unique value come alive.

So, just as some people are extolling the value of rites of recognition to properly note the achievement of elderhood, we urge you all to recognize and admire the old people in the midst of this community-in-formation. Recognizing each other is recognizing Creation at work here, locally, in all of our lives.

This is a significant part of what we as a community of old people have to give each other. Recognizing each other is recognizing oneself.

੨੦

Personal and Transpersonal

— Lucky

I'm fond of saying that community dances upon two legs. If, it gives too much attention to either, it falls over. The two legs, at least in my mind, are the personal and the transpersonal. Too much reliance on either creates imbalance; not enough of either creates a lame community.

By transpersonal I mean that which goes through and beyond each of us, the sense that there is some kind of spirit at work in our connection. This can be a feeling or some kind of other perception. It most often occurs in groups as a feeling of inexplicable interrelatedness. I tend to like it. It feels fairly rare. It can be a hiding place. One can refuse to meet the otherness of others there. Community can tip over with too much reliance on this aspect of who we are. It is possible for it to be too impersonal.

Therefore the personal is really important. Any real sense of connection arises from feeling known for and as oneself and being realistically cared about. Community cannot really support, challenge, contradict, or affirm anyone without this personal dimension. In my experience, this knowing is where commitment comes from. Too much emphasis upon the personal unbalances the other way though. People need to have the chance to show up voluntarily in their own way. This is where trusting in and knowing the transpersonal becomes a real necessity.

The tyranny that most of us have experienced in groups and communities has largely been because of the rigid overemphasis upon one or the other.

The experience of community has to do with the feeling of caring that is going around. This caring is a hallmark of an elder community. It may not arise at first in a general way, that is, as a widespread feeling while being with the group. It could happen at first, like it did with our original Elders Salon, with a specific feeling of caring for a single person. In our situation it was the open-heart surgery and recovery of one of us that helped us realize what had changed in our hearts.

Caring is often a gift of the old. All of the growth that comes with hardships, expanded perspective, and relationship make it possible for us older folks to care as never before. What we have held primarily for our grandkids or the Earth, we can give to each other. Community and caring in general arise out of the vulnerability of being human together. The public revelation of our shared vulnerability is galvanizing. Risk being true to yourself, and you will find you are not alone in caring about the risk of living with your heart open.

Caring is palpable. People don't need to guess about it. It is a feeling, which means it can be felt. Connection with significant others is a gift, a gift that often comes in strange forms. To receive it one often has to open oneself through pain and disappointment. It takes courage to care, or to allow oneself to be cared about. This kind of courage sometimes is years in the making and is encouraged by the proximity of death. It is more likely amongst us old folks. Nevertheless, caring must be earned. Open up — not just the easy parts; give each other the hard parts to hold. Oddly, community caring comes about when enough people show their tender hearts to each other. Old folks know more than most what this entails. Elder community arises because the old practice revealing themselves to each other.

In a real community, the tide of caring rises and falls. The transpersonal, by virtue of it being bigger than the individual, is more unconditional. It is often perceived as a spiritual kind of caring, based upon the fact of existence. Personal caring is more conditional — often based upon how one exists.

Both are necessary. To feel really cared about one has to feel known (the personal). To feel cared about, no matter what, requires a sure sense that one is valued for one's existence (the transpersonal). Caring rises and falls as the personal and transpersonal are balanced and re-balanced. Elders know something about self-care, (these two elements need to be balanced within too) and paradoxically that's what gives elders the capacity to care for others.

The real benefit of creating elder community together, of caring about each other, is that there is no better way to discover the potential that resides in the human heart. When one directly experiences connection, when one knows in a palpable form the truth of what binds us to ourselves, one another, and this earth, then one is confidently free. This freedom comes from within and is demonstrated without. With freedom one can be authentically true to oneself, to Life, and to others.

Paradox

— *Lucky*

This little piece is not really about growing an elder community. You may have noticed that much of this handbook has to do with acknowledging elder skills. There is a whole lot about elder life that isn't known or appropriately understood. This ignorance about the potentials of the old, much of it cultural, limits the way old people see themselves (and their possibilities), each other, and the world. An important piece of how awareness changes with age is the advent of paradoxical awareness.

Connection has a more fluid feel at this stage of life. Things are both discrete (clearly themselves) and permeable (melted into each other). There is a greater complexity that has become a greater simplicity. The rational and the irrational exist side by side. Life flows with a vitality that moves in ways that are unimaginable. Reality has a life of its own. The transcendent speaks through paradox in ways that delight and mystify. The elder knows him or herself as a grown child. Innocence has more shrewdly returned.

Life in the paradoxical lane is more expansive for having its limits. This sense slowly infiltrates the awareness of the old — changing everything — and leaving everything alone. An increase in perspective, in behavioral options, becomes available, but in no way like before. Life enters more fully and seems to have its own language, and paradox is a part of it. Life includes a strange sheen of meaning that defies thought, and compels wonder. Reverence and humility reveal how much this aspect of Life has entered awareness.

This is an experience one cannot conjure up. No amount of years, workshops, spiritual practice, meditation, or effort can achieve this awareness. It is part of human potential but is only activated by Life for its own reasons. Lightening falls on the heads of some who, like or not, are selected as emissaries, the most ripened fruit. Paradox is a form of lightening — one that quickens the mix. Some old people are blown open in this way. They become elders, but really they are Evolution incarnate.

As aging proceeds, for some people a kind of grace takes over. Something larger moves, and one is incorporated into a new, very different, reality. All is changed. This shift may have been years in the making; it may have seemed highly unlikely and random; but here it is, right on time. The world comes to Life in a new way, and the miraculous suddenly becomes palpable.

Some old folks become elders. They have no claim on anything. They are broken down, sickly, weak, and addled, yet they see very clearly. Some kind of larger mind now occupies them. This isn't the invasion of an alien awareness; this is the best of what it means to be human. They have pulled off the seemingly impossible. They have become themselves *and* the Universe, all at once. Or, so it seems. But, in fact, they are aging into it, ripening, and little by little becoming quintessentially what we all are.

This shift doesn't happen overnight. It takes the vagaries of Life, hardships, a great deal of paradox, and a long ripening time. The miracle is that just as the caterpillar enters the chrysalis and the butterfly emerges, an old person can be transformed too. Add to that miracle — the rebirth of Life — a transformed perspective, and you have a rare kind of metamorphosis, the kind that can change a whole species.

As I've said, aspects of elder awareness do not appear all at once; they slowly emerge. A growing appreciation for paradox accompanies the advent and development of this change. There is also a strong sense of relationship that can mark the beginning. This can start with an increased attachment and identification with grandchildren, but quickly advances to others' grandchildren and on to young people in general, other humans, and nature. Just as wrinkles, weight, and greyness slowly appear, this new and strange perception takes its time. It is a surprise that until now hasn't been seen and appropriately valued — by greying individuals or by our culture. Let us hope that this time of terrible waste is now over.

I've tried to make the point that a new possibility is on the horizon. The greying of the populace is likely to remake the world. The shift in the populace is going to throw us. The qualitative shift in awareness is going to transform us. *How* remains to be seen, but I think it fair to look at the qualities of this new form of awareness for guidance. Remember, what is emerging is more connective, paradoxical, emotional, and experiential. These attributes offer us cues. The future is unfolding.

Ultimately, the reason for this section is that elder community is a natural incubator for new kinds of consciousness or awareness. These developments are needed both for us old folks and for a world that is suffering from our species' immaturity. The old, if they can awaken their capacities for connection, offer a form of maturity that is sorely needed. This awakening is natural. It happens as we age. If one participates in the birthing of an elder community, one will see it for oneself. Paradoxical awareness shows up.

Elder community is a place where the miracle of "hatching out" takes place — a bunch of grey youth are born. This is, in itself, a very paradoxical happening, but it isn't the most paradoxical thing. It marks the beginning of what could be a larger transformation. The greater paradox becomes visible in an elder community. There one can see that Life reduces us through sickness, aging, and all manner of hardship, while simultaneously enlarging us. Life, while corralling us with our limitations, draws out of us what is greatest and most essential in our nature. Alexandra and I call this phenomenon reduction, though it is really Life growing us, improving its product.

Happiness and elder fulfillment are a more widespread possibility. Just rubbing shoulders with old people regularly and knowing what to look for, frees us and makes for some new possible ways of being older. Life has cooked up this paradox, one that releases new meaning. Now Life could use our help to midwife this transformation.

At the Center

— *Lucky*

There is another thing that should be alluded to. Words cannot really convey the significance or power of this phenomenon, but it cannot go unreferenced. As a group begins to form, as people begin to bond, something else is at work. It is the thing that calls together a group and makes it jell. I am referring to an invisible, but palpable, presence, which acts like gravity and pulls everything together. Something sits at the heart of all communities.

I'm not writing this to be dramatic or to be mystical; I'm writing it to be real. Any forming elders' group is going to be aided by an invisible force that exists in some way. Who gets pulled into the circle is never random. There is an intelligence that forms as the group does. It constellates as the group takes shape and acts to assist in a group's development.

So far I have managed to avoid spiritual terms, though some people who read this may already be going in that direction. Those kinds of reverential attitudes make sense to me, but I am loath to reduce this phenomenon to that alone. This may be a natural phenomenon, brought on by our social nature. There is something that actively participates in the evolution of community. Something that has power, that seems to care, that uses all interactions, no matter how small and seemingly inconsequential, to help growth and evolution occur.

I think of it as a collective life form, made up of all the aspiration, feelings, savvy, heartaches, and other vivid experiences of the participants in the group. I tend to think of this mystery as a greater social being, more tuned in to the big picture than any one of us can be alone. Whatever it is — call it a mystery — I have learned that it exists at another level. I believe this power can be relied on; it will work to make a group of strangers into a viable community.

Along the way it needs to be fed, like all organisms, but because it is a collective being, composed of human qualities, its food is us. Paradoxically, it feeds us in return. We feed it by going beyond ourselves, by being vulnerable, by showing our quivering, naked, humanness to each other. It feeds us by giving us back to ourselves, enlarged, more connected, and more filled with life. Community and elders thrive when this interaction is takes place.

So, there is something, some would say some kind of spirit, that resides at the very center of a community. I tend to think that this "being" is what makes a community a healing, wholing place. Honoring what is, constellated by coming together, empowers what happens, which then rebounds to the benefit of all and our larger world. In the final analysis, one of the reasons I believe that growing an elder community takes no special skills is because there is something greater than any one of us that is doing the real community-building.

A Note on Spirituality

— Alexandra

Ritual, spiritual practices, and the like are inherently part of our experience as we age, but they must be separated from belief systems in a differentiated population. This can be awkward and difficult to accomplish because individual language, belief, and religious thought are idiosyncratic to such a large degree. In creating group experiences that can be acceptable to an elder community, specific systems must be avoided at the same time reverence, gratitude, and acknowledgment of something of the unknown or Mystery, as I sometimes identify it, is included.

I particularly like the use of "Life" as a term for the motivating force because it clearly is present in us all at the same time as it clearly springs from something greater than the individual. This avoids the problem of theistic identifications and can be acceptable to an atheistic point of view and a nondual or theistic view as well. I am grateful to Lucky's book *Embracing Life* for this noncontroversial way of holding what might otherwise be called God, the Unknown, or the Mystery.

ॐ

Free and Freedom

— Lucky

Alexandra and I stumbled upon something, which has turned out to become one of the most important facets of the Elders Salon. By virtue of having a public place to meet that was large and accommodating and that we didn't have to rent, we learned, over the years, that having the meetings (and peripheral activities of the salon) be free of cost has impacted the likelihood of creating a caring community. Being free has done several things for the development of trust, comradery, and brought home the transitional nature of what we are doing. The absence of money has made the real value of an elders' community more evident and accessible.

The fact that no one profits (in monetary terms) from our getting together has set up some important dynamics. One of our members said it best: "Caring is our currency." The salon has become the home for an extra-economic valuing — of ourselves, each other, and what we are doing together. Happily for all of us we discovered this way to go beyond cultural values to real values. This is the heart of the transitional nature of the salon.

Right now, community is being built through caring, voluntary feelings aroused by real situations and real people. The goal of increasing community resilience, a Transition value, we have learned happens best when people feel known and cared about, when their bonds are emotional not economical. It also helps to prevent a hierarchy among us, making our sense of being peers more palpable.

This economic independence fits nicely with the surge toward freedom that comes with growing older. Old people need to become themselves — it's now or never! Death is coming into view; there is little time to waste. Interactions now must satisfy a hunger for meaning, not just cognitive meaning. A good lecture is only partially satisfying; but now, by virtue of aging, the hunger is for the meaning of personal existence. For this sense of meaning to unfold, old people need to be free; they need to discover themselves for themselves. They need to find out what is within them.

Throughout this handbook we emphasize the importance of freedom, especially for older folks. There is a drive that comes from within (I call it evolution), to fulfill oneself. And fulfillment is entirely idiosyncratic. There are similarities in the growth patterns of old people, but each one has his or her own form. Building a community that honors this full range of diversity is challenging and highly rewarding. Freedom makes it work.

The door must be open. Folks need to be free to come and go. People need to know they can be different — because, in fact, they are. Inclusivity must permeate the atmosphere. By emphasizing the freedom to be and discover oneself, old people gravitate toward a social environment where they can share the experience of being older, experiment with freedom, and discover themselves, often through one another. Old people become elders through knowing themselves, each other, and Life well. The gift that each is can only be given freely, and life in a community where diversity is honored empowers that giving.

Every social organization that tries to be congenial to freedom is confronted with the same challenge. All social organisms require structure, but structure can be the enemy of freedom. Most of us have found ourselves captured by, or caught outside of, these structures. Boundaries are essential to community, and they threaten freedom. How this paradox is handled will determine how congenial any community will be.

The urge to be true to oneself has proven to be complicated in the past. There has been too much conformity or too thorough a rejection. This means that when a group of older people are brought together, there must be some diligent effort made by the hosting team to demonstrate balance. The group defines boundaries for itself and becomes the community of its choosing. The host team's job is to keep the group creating a structure that ensures inclusivity, the freedom to be oneself.

Freedom has not often been the goal of most communities, but to serve the developmental needs of old folks and to increase the probability of the old becoming elders, then freedom has to be a core value. The evolution of elder community depends upon it. The freedom to be oneself is the building block that allows caring about others to evolve. There is no caring about others if there is no caring about oneself. The freedom to discover and be oneself, therefore, is intrinsic to caring community.

Play

— *Lucky*

The attitude of play (playfulness) is available to old folks in a way that it has never been before. This is some kind of miracle because it can ensure happiness, but the miraculousness of it is not readily apparent. Childhood had its moments of play. They were important. It has even been said that "play is a child's form of work." So much is learned there about the environment, cultural roles, fun, and being human. Play, especially in children, looks frivolous, but isn't. All of our mammalian ancestors played — for good reason. Play seems to be one of the most effective and fun ways to express, and then discover, the self's capabilities. It is nature's way.

Old folks go through some important phases in their development that are like childhood. One psychologist referred to being older as a time of "emancipated innocence." Play is as important to elder becoming as it is to kids. However, play has a bad reputation for adults. Even though substantial developmental work is happening, under the cover of fun — play is often looked down upon. This has the effect of making play, an instinctive way towards growth, a complex experience for adults.

Older adults often suffer from the same kind of play prejudices that prevail in our culture. Play is too often viewed as frivolous, unproductive and a waste of time. These prejudices, I believe, lie on the same continuum of prejudice that includes ageism. Both old people, and play, are seen as unproductive and valueless. This view of play (and the old), which unfortunately, prevails in our culture, makes play (and aging) a complicated and ambivalent experience for many adults.

The way towards freedom for elders, however, is through play. The liberating effect of being able to try out a variety of roles, coping strategies, and ways of being that are fun, is enormous. When one cultivates an attitude of playfulness, it is easier to meet each situation creatively, looking for the opportunity for fun and self-expression. Self-discovery accompanies play. So, endeavor to cultivate an attitude of play.

Play, despite cultural assumptions, comes pretty naturally to old folks. Play is the way our natural selves manifest. It is noticeable in the way old people interact, inquire into differences, joke, and seek meaning together. Encourage this. Enjoy! Praise it when you notice it. Participating in the emergence of elder community is fun. So is being free to be yourself. Play at it! Enjoy the moments when it is really clear how good it is to be alive, and growing older, in this confusing era.

On Playfulness

—Alexandra

I'd like to add a few thoughts here. Play is one of the very best ways to make new discoveries, whether as a child, an inventor, an artist, or at any age. It opens and relaxes the mind, enlivens the spirit, releases tensions about performance, improves one's attitude, and frees one up generally. It teaches and entertains. No wonder healthcare folks tell us that laughing is curative!

One caveat is that a non-rule of successful play is that there can only be rules that are agreed to on the spot by the participants and that one can't be forced to play and still call it "play." It must be freely engaged in. So, I'm engaged in a playful endeavor to discover just what it is that elder play is made up of. So far it seems to have a range from foolishness to seriously, playfully, deep inquiry, mostly centered in verbal interplay, but not excluding some slapstick.

It's difficult to overcome cultural biases against play for adults: for example, a member of a younger generation may say of an older person, "S/he is going into a second childhood!" Playfulness and foolishness can result in negative branding unless the recipient is savvy enough to turn the tables, not take it personally or be emotionally reactive, possibly get playful in response, or in some way just not allow "crooked thinking" (as my father would call it) to hold sway.

৵

Taking Care of Oneself

— Lucky

There is wide-spread awe and fear of the effects of our culture. Some people talk about it as a toxic culture, meaning that it necessarily has a corrosive effect upon everyone. While I might agree with seeing our present-time culture in this way, I don't agree with the sentiment that follows. It is possible to develop a kind of immunity to the prevailing zeitgeist. In fact, this is a major benefit of development.

Growing more complex and capable than what passes for the norm in one's culture-of- origin is an attribute of Life. It is one goal of growth and development. Despite the popular notion (which is made from earlier stages of development) that what is external — like family or culture — defines one's possibilities, Life disagrees. The inner life — particularly growth and development — provides freedom from culture and immunity to its siren call.

The real issue in this culture, western industrialized society, is that there is little support and awareness for the value of learning to take care of oneself in relationship. Many people don't even know this is desirable or possible. Taking care of oneself in relationship doesn't seem relevant in a fragmented world. The assumption that the fragmenting effects of modern culture outweigh the constant relatedness of Life and eclipse connectedness leaves too many people unprepared for the real complexity of Life and unaware of the capacity (and need) to take care of oneself in relationship.

Psychology has worked hard to show the value of boundaries in the process of growing a self of one's own. Unfortunately, this has been primarily interpreted to be about safety. Again, an earlier form of development (mostly one focused on minimizing the risks from outside sources) has shaped the worldview that prevails in our culture. This is only partially true. Boundaries are at least as important for self-definition and self-regulation as they are for moderating outside threats.

At later, more self-regulating stages of development, boundaries are for the originator rather than for others. Boundaries at this level are for facing and acknowledging one's own limitations rather than another's. Without self-knowledge and self-regard it is impossible to take care of oneself relationally. Boundaries transform themselves from being about safety and fear to being about self-growth and love. The better one can take care of oneself in relationship, the greater one's capacity for loving.

Learning to take care of oneself in a community is like learning to take care of oneself in any social situation or the world. The diversity and size of a community means that at any meeting one is likely to experience the "unknown other." This is the person, or people, one is most likely to project fear upon. That stranger, or the one who seems most dangerously like the one who previously delivered hurt, will most likely represent one's anxiety. When these "others" are seen or otherwise experienced, one tends to clench up or otherwise disappear.

This is one of those moments when one is likely to give up or lose oneself. This is also a moment when one has learned to be afraid and to take care of oneself badly. Thus, community offers a place that is uncomfortable in just the way one needs to learn how to take care in.

This is one of the saving rigors of learning community. It has within it the kind of support one needs to be true to oneself, meaning the right level of social affirmation, while providing one with the exact level of challenge one needs to prove to oneself that one can stay true to oneself. The situation of social diversity that an open elder community provides serves to deliver the exact amount of challenging "otherness" that facilitates development of self.

This is where one's freedom to be true to oneself lies. It is the place where one can, if one has the courage and desire, learn to take care of oneself. This is a revolutionary act. Culture, no matter where one came from, is no longer king. Activism, of all sorts, becomes loving instead of reactive and full of fear. The world we live in is transformed. The possibility that love and sanity can prevail in an insane and seemingly loveless world is now afoot. The world is cared for better when we learn how better to take care of ourselves.

If one can be free wherever one is, then one can be as loving as one likes. If one has it within them to always, in all circumstances, be true to oneself, then Life is not a problem to be solved — it is a miracle to be experienced. Taking care of oneself in relationship opens many doors. Elders can surprise the world by walking through some of them.

Becoming an Elder

— Lucky

How is it that an old person becomes someone rare, an elder? Elder community is designed to assist one into maturing. Through interacting with one's age cohort and sharing how time and Life have changed one, a discovery can happen of what nature has wrought within. This discovery begins the transition, a metamorphosis that alters one's outlook and choices.

An elder is grown. Like sperm cells on the way to the ovum, they are the few that have run the gauntlet of Life, and been altered. They are blessed by hard-won experience, hardship, and perspective, not because they survived (as many an old person does), but because they learned to thrive. Elders are amongst the precious few who have lived through the spectrum of Life and become the ripest of the ripe.

How is an elder different from being a merely old person? An elder is not defined by age. He, or she, is old, but they are not subject to time in the same way the majority of us are. They have a repertoire of responses to it and capacities that reveal what they are made of. Here is what I mean.

Elders arrive at old age differently than the average old person. They are more self-possessed, more interested in others, less emotionally reactive and judgmental, more compassionate, and eager to serve the larger communities they feel themselves to be part of. They are motivated more from the inside out rather than the outside in. They are more self-confrontive and treat themselves and Life better. They know what their purpose is. Elders are humble; they know they are older and wiser because of life experiences and hardships. They are who they are because Life made them that way. They are the ones who have learned the alchemical trick of turning lemons into joyous lives.

Elders embrace challenge because they recognize its role in Life. They are familiar with loss, hardship, and pain. They have been grown by what they have been through. Life has treated them roughly, and they are better off for it. As a result they have a different outlook on difficulty and a different capacity for dealing with it. They can feel confident about Life because it has put them to the test.

They have a rare ability to respond that sets them apart. Unlike others, elders consider and take responsibility for the groups they feel part of. They know that the challenges of Life coax out of us, as individuals and as groups, the ability to respond. They personally increase a group's ability to respond by changing themselves.

Growing is organic. There is an inescapable storm-surge that runs through all of our lives. Change is ubiquitous, it is always happening. Our best-laid plans, the well-ordered lives we imagine for ourselves, the world we thought we lived in, all morph into something else. Our grip is slippery. Life twists and turns, and we are whiplashed around. Change seems to happen for its own sake. In fact, this is true. Evolution is shaking things up. It is looking for new combinations which will allow it to complexify, to become more functional, and even more greatly creative. In the meantime, we get buffeted around.

Elders, however, have the winds of evolution behind them. They have extraordinary experiences of transcending themselves. They go beyond the ruts, old ways, and attachments that have previously defined them. They have the experience, not always voluntary, of having given up control. They know that death awaits them and that it can take many forms. They have adjusted to the restless and ever-changing nature of Life. They are distinguishable from the merely old because they have not become rigid. They know how to dance amidst transition. They have made friends with change by expecting it, celebrating it, and leaning into it.

Elders have gained access to the wisdom of the ages because Life has had its way with them. They are evolution at work. Becoming an elder is not simply done. The journey to elderhood is made purely at Life's discretion. There are broader laws to adhere to, community to be responsible for, and a relationship with the larger mystery to maintain. All of this is an extension of human capacity. But, the way there isn't rational or even logical.

All one can do is position oneself to be selected by Life. Until now this has been a kind of random process, at least on the human side. Some show us, however, another possibility. This is the most important reason elder community exists: so we can learn from each other, as we age, the attributes that make a human life nutritious to the whole. The big picture, a larger reality, comes into view in the latter stages of life.

Occupying this world as fully as possible (and bringing along one's community) is what life is all about. Evolution proceeds by its own reasons. Some folks have learned to trust this apparent randomness as an expression of Life's wisdom. They have become elders, and they are the way-showers, the ones that reveal our possibilities.

Blossoming, fruiting, and becoming seed — this is what old people can do. A community of those on the same trajectory is more than just helpful. The relationship capabilities of the old are not just a convenience that enriches life. These capacities serve to help old people become fully ripe human beings. A community of elderly people can become a nutrient-rich container that sensitizes, fertilizes, and grows a rare experience of purpose. The old contain the wisdom, experience, and perspective that can enable change.

Becoming an elder is a ripening process, a privilege given to one by Life. By becoming the grey fruit of the Tree of Life, one seeds the future. This is not an intentional act. This is an outgrowth of Life having its way with us. Elders know this, and are therefore humble and vulnerable. They are distinguished from the merely old because they have given their lives to the whole of Life. Community is the place where one discovers and practices being oneself while learning how being oneself is exactly what is needed now.

Summary

— Lucky

Writing down something as important as how we old folks connect is a real challenge. When I started out with the salon I had no idea these strangers were going to affect me so strongly. Now, I'm so grateful they have. I want to do right by them and what I have learned with them. There is so much I didn't know: about me, others, and the world. Congregating with and caring about old folks has awakened me. So, writing this handbook has been educational. Reflecting on the journey, I've been made clearer about what a boon old age is to old folks and, even more, to a world desperately needing perspective.

I'm getting excited about this handbook. It seems very different to me, different from all the other "elder" books, because it affirms the fact that we as old people can create a way of being together that is free from culture, expertise, and all the do-gooders who are ready to give us their formulas on who we are and can be. Wisdom resides in our experiences, not in things outside us. Let's relate and find out for ourselves.

It is my lasting pleasure to be so engaged. Old folks on the way to becoming elders; this is an incredible resource. The word has gotten out. There is a longevity revolution happening, and it is combining with a demographic shift (the baby-boomers are coming), so there is a fairly large supply of people who are excited and want to tell us old folks how to be. But we aren't done becoming yet. The wheel is still spinning; evolution is still shaping our possibilities; it is too soon to settle. We need each other to find out what is possible with us. Elder community is a path to freedom, to becoming truly ourselves, and I hope some folks will feel moved to care about what we can be for each other, the world, and ourselves.

For My Part...

— *Alexandra*

This handbook section has represented the cooperative venture that Lucky and I engaged in while creating the Transition Sebastopol Elders Salon and associated activities. The "Deeper In" portion that follows is taken from other writing and experiences that Lucky has gathered up to enrich your community-building experience.

Growing older has been one of the most surprising rides of my life, these last few years since I suffered the loss of my husband, my home, my life as I had been living it. All this has successfully grown me into a far more emotionally intelligent, less reactive, more caring, better differentiated person. This began with me speaking very gently and sweetly to myself when I made mistakes or lost track of things shortly after his death. I began to care better for myself, which then made it easy to care for everything in a deeper way.

That this time of my life surpasses any other period for sheer ongoing happiness seems impossible! It hasn't had the thrills, the ups and the downs of younger life; it's a much quieter inner experience of satisfaction, peace, feeling that I fit in, that my life has meaning. This is due in large part to balancing my own solitude with the richness of a community life peopled with many older, wiser beings than I'd ever stopped to encounter previously.

Therefore, my hope for you readers is that you will find your own peace and delight in your wisdom years, challenges and all, and that what we've shared with you here may help you discover more riches and contribute to a more fully developed life.

My greater hope is that this unusual convergence of people with a longer life expectancy combined with the demographics of so many elders alive at the same time may begin to tip the balance toward wisdom, and shift our world culture toward caring more deeply and more wisely toward all Life.

॰॰

DEEPER IN

Grow old with me!
The best is yet to be, the last of life
for which the first was made."
— *Robert Browning*

GUIDELINES

As for old age, embrace and love it. It abounds
with pleasure if you know how to use it.
The gradually declining years
are among the sweetest of life...."
— Seneca

Angeles Arrien, the Four-Fold Way

—Lucky

Angeles Arrien was born in the Pyrénnés. She is Basque. She was raised partly in the Pyrénnés, and partly in Idaho. This bi-cultural experience turned into a life-long interest in multiculturalism. When she went to college at U.C. Berkeley she found that the field of Anthropolgy gave her the best chance to express her multicultural interests.

Thank the Mystery it did! Out of her studies of the world's spiritual traditions she was able to identify four commonalities. These four practices universally inform us and provide a method for all humans to maximize their potential.

I recommend the four practices that follow as the backbone of building a rapport with each other, that allows the fullness of our individual gifts, and helps convert them into precious collective capabilities. The Four-Fold Way is:

- *Show up and Choose to be Present*
- *Pay Attention to what has heart and meaning*
- *Tell the Truth without blame*
- *Surrender Attachment to Outcome*

I refer to them as practices much like movements in martial arts. If given a chance, through practice, they will deliver one to new levels of mastery and connection. When practiced together, they have the uncanny power to create social synergies that deliver groups to finer and finer sensibilities.

The Four-Fold Way:
Practices for Transformational Learning
—Lucky

The overarching principles we employ with learning communities are found in the Four-Fold Way developed by cultural anthropologist Angeles Arrien. Studying patterns of psycho-spiritual practice across many different cultures, she identified four universal components: showing up and choosing to be present, paying attention, telling the truth, and surrendering attachment to an outcome.

The large group provides a social vehicle for change and its built-in diversity generates energy. The Four-Fold Way harnesses this energy and utilizes it to propel the members and the group as a whole into new realms of perception and behavior.

A learning community's process transports the group from one view of reality to another, from one form of social orientation to a larger, more encompassing social framework. This kind of learning does not proceed solely through informational training or through the acquisition of skills, but through transformation — the "emptying out" of an established mindset and immersion in a different experience.

As the group explores the tensions associated with community and diversity, it becomes evident that there are no ready, formulaic solutions to these tensions. Participants may well despair about finding a way through these tensions. Remarkably, when they learn how to hang out with their limitations, they come to the place where they become sensitized and discover genuinely new possibilities.

Showing Up and Choosing to Be Present
The first element of the Four-Fold Way — showing up and choosing to be present — describes a minimum requirement for transformation. Nevertheless, it is an exacting practice, involving much more than simply being physically present. Showing up means making yourself

known — taking a position by communicating what matters to you about yourself, and your experiences in the group and the world. In Arrien's words, showing up requires discipline in the sense of being "a disciple to the self."

Making oneself visible can be anxiety provoking. Many people assume that community means support and confirmation. This may be true in a community of affinity. In a large and diverse group however, one learns very rapidly that whatever one expresses is likely to be met with a range of responses, including contradiction and conflict. There are no guarantees that others will understand, agree with, value or validate what is disclosed. Thus, showing up requires striving for self-definition, self-advocacy and self-expression in the face of disconfirming responses from those who see things differently. To continue to fully show up members must learn how to validate their own reality without withdrawing from interactions with those who differ. This learning takes time. Members must discover how to manage their anxiety about differing with others, so that they can make the contributions to the group that are theirs to make, by virtue of their unique perspective.

As the group matures it becomes clear that something other than a capacity to take a position and assert a viewpoint is necessary for learning to occur. This is where choosing to be present becomes important. Presence means making oneself available to be touched and changed by others. This entails opening oneself to bear witness to others' perspectives, to listen attentively and respectfully, and to be shaped by the variety of contributions others make toward the development of the group. It also means experiencing what is painful, difficult, or incomplete in oneself and in the group.

Choosing to be present asks participants to stay engaged with a process that is beyond their singular control, to share responsibility for what occurs within the group. This challenges the tendency many have to wait for someone else to create an environment that "allows" them to reveal themselves. The goal is not to create special, "hothouse" environments that protect people from the anxieties and risks of taking their own unique positions. Instead a learning community provides a social context where individuals learn to master themselves so that they can tolerate the possibility of conflict or discomfort in order to make their own unique contributions to the community's process. Showing up and choosing to be present is an essential practice in creating community through diversity. It challenges members to bring themselves ever more completely into play, and, in the process, to reveal and sustain the experience of diversity in the group. As the members become more proficient at showing up and choosing to be present, they enter the realm of paradoxical tensions that can provide passage to a new way of being together.

Paying Attention

Paying attention is an essential practice without which transformative learning cannot occur. A distinguishing characteristic of a learning community is the quality of consciousness, or attention, that members bring to the task of being together. Increasing awareness sensitizes our perceptions and introduces increasingly subtle levels of reality — and this is what changes the participants.

In the formative stages of a learning community we encourage members to pay particular attention to tension — in oneself and in the group. Since the goal in a learning community is to move toward inclusion and connection, the focus is particularly on the tensions that exist between inclusion and exclusion, and between connection and separation. Observing these tensions helps group members recognize their own struggles with differing and with responding to otherness.

The first tension — between inclusion and exclusion — has to do with who or what is encompassed within the group, and who or what is considered unacceptable or outside the boundaries of awareness. The fundamental questions underlying this tension are: "How much differing can be tolerated?" and "How can I (or others) tolerate the uncertainty aroused by differing realities?" Exclusion decreases diversity, therefore diminishing anxiety, but also limits the scope of the group's potential for learning. On the other hand, inclusion increases anxiety in the group as new information challenges comfortable assumptions and demands the formulation of a more complex picture of reality.

When reality confronts a group (or individual) with more diversity than it can handle, the typical unconscious response is to try to reduce diversity — the encounter with otherness — through excluding part of reality: either one's own reality, another's reality, or the relationship between these realities. Excluding one's own reality occurs when participants devalue their own viewpoints, hide or silence aspects of themselves, forget what is important to them, are dishonest with themselves or the group, or wait for others to give them permission to make their own contributions (to be themselves). Taking oneself out of the picture minimizes the possibility of differing or conflicting with someone else. It also undermines the feeling of belonging and gives the group an incomplete reality from which to operate. This attempt to minimize diversity tension feeds cultural dynamics such as the segregation and marginalization of those who lack social rank — ethnic minorities, the old and disabled, children, etc.

Excluding another's reality happens when group members try to impose their own perspective on others. This can occur through direct argument and denigration, but it can also happen through persuasion, teaching, healing, analyzing, converting, sympathizing, pitying, generalizing, and asserting rigid rules or "right ways" for participating in community. This attempt to minimize diversity tension feeds and reflects cultural dynamics such as political correctness, fundamentalism, ideological imperialism and ethnic cleansing.

Excluding the relationship means devaluing the significance of contact and denying the fact that every participant has something unique to contribute. In this case there is an attempt to minimize the impact of encounter by pretending that there is nothing held in common or no way of making a meaningful exchange. This form of exclusion may take the form of abrupt silent withdrawals from membership or a refusal to engage. Slogans such as "You do your thing, I'll do mine," "We'll agree to disagree," "My way, or the highway," all reflect this pattern. On a cultural political level this pattern is reflected in the self-marginalization of militia groups, cults and isolationistic national policies.

Each of these forms of exclusion is a way of reducing existential uncertainty by trying to maintain the illusion that there is only one reality, rather than multiple co-existing versions of reality. These responses to differences are toxic to the vitality of a learning community — as well as to social, political, global communities — because they limit the potential for the evolution of new awareness. Observing these tendencies increases awareness of the underlying roots of many painful cultural dynamics, such as racism, sexism, ethnic conflict, and environmental abuse. As awareness grows members begin to perceive the parallels between personal choices and group dynamics. They experientially understand the origins of some of the worst symptoms of diversity intolerance. They also discover how their own choices contribute to either reinforcing or altering these dynamics.

Another focal point for attention to the social koan is the dynamic tension that exists between separation and connection. Here paying attention means focusing upon how we maintain separation and cultivate connection, and observing what actually happens within oneself and in the group. "How do I maintain separation?" "When and how do I experience connection?" "When does there seem to be an atmosphere of connection in the group?"

One of the common notions about connection is that it follows from safety. In a learning community members discover that actions taken for self-protection usually obstruct contact and generate an atmosphere of distrust within the individual and the group. Members begin to observe how defensive behaviors are often offensive to others. With this awareness comes the realization that our attempts to preserve personal security frequently block us from the sense of connection with others, that maintaining safety (in the sense of invulnerability to others) perpetuates separation rather than connection.

Similarly, as participants pay attention to the actual experience of connection, they are often surprised to find that it arises precisely from situations that might be prejudged as "unsafe." For instance, conflict often feels threatening at first as it highlights the diversity and autonomy of the members. However, as participants use conflict to deepen their positions and presence in the group, they find that they feel more connected and that the group becomes more inclusive. The deepest bonds often arise from the deepest differing.

Another significant awareness regarding separation and connection has to do with the notion that we connect with each other based upon expertise, accomplishment, status or strengths. In the learning community process, participants are asked to reflect on the ways in which role, rank and status affect group dynamics and the nature of connection. While accomplishment is valuable, it can also impede the deepest levels of connection based on shared humanity. One of the paradoxes of the social koan is that we must simultaneously bring all of who we are to the interactions, while temporarily suspending our roles and customary identities.

As a group works together over time, the practice of paying attention generates a form of group awareness, or mindfulness. Observing and reflecting upon the group's "thinking process," members begin noticing their own judgments and preconceptions. This is important because our assumptions are invisible lenses that filter our perceptions and separate us from direct experience. The practice of identifying, examining, and suspending assumptions arouses awareness of the relativity of our perceptions, reminding us that our preconceptions determine what we observe. This practice leads to the fundamental recognition that differing assumptions underlie our relationships and account for much of the confusion and conflict we experience with each other. Paying attention to the effects of our assumptions generates an open and observant form of attention that allows a fresh sense of discernment.

The growing mindfulness of the group reveals the subtle interconnections encompassing individual behavior, interpersonal relations, group processes and cultural dynamics. The group's attention becomes more focused, creating awareness that is both more penetrating, revealing the nuances of a particular issue, and more encompassing, revealing the larger patterns of which the components are a part. Larger realms of meaning, ordinarily beyond the awareness of a single individual, become accessible. Cultivating this kind of awareness is hard and complicated work. The large group process, with its built-in social diversity, creates both the necessity for developing these attentional capacities and also the training ground where they can be fostered.

Telling the Truth

Transformational learning proceeds through the acquisition of a more accurate and comprehensive perception of reality. Telling the truth, like the other elements of the Four-Fold-Way, introduces us to unanticipated dimensions of reality.

In a learning community, as in life, the practice of telling the truth starts with discerning one's own position and viewpoint. Truth telling is a way of making one's reality available to become part of the wisdom of the group. As members open up to each other, it becomes clear that truth is far more complicated than any individual's singular perspective.

The emergence of a multifaceted sense of truth is disturbing and leads into the volatile heart of the diversity dilemma. It forces us to confront the realization that our reality is relative — one among many constructed perspectives. The experience of truth's complexity creates a kind of chaos, a cognitive dissonance that disassembles and disorients. Familiar reality is unraveled and we are thrust into an open space where what was once true is now seen as limited. One's reality is both deconstructed and reconstructed by exposure to unfamiliar truths.

Avoiding disturbing truths happens (psychologically and culturally) through two core patterns — denial and indulgence. We practice denial when we insist on the truth that has served us previously and refuse to see what currently is true, or when we deny the realities of others because we fear that we cannot handle the demands new truths will make upon us. We practice indulgence when we dramatize or sensationalize our particular sense of truth, insisting that it is the truth rather than a truth. In each case we want to avoid experiencing our truth's incompleteness because we fear losing the comfort, security and equilibrium we find in it. As these patterns occur in the large group, participants find themselves stretched between two desires: on the one hand, shielding themselves from the stress of opening to new realities, and, on the other hand, optimizing their learning and connection in the group. Within this tension, transformation occurs, as participants develop greater tolerance for complexity and paradox.

Sharing a multi-faceted experience of the moment makes significantly more of the wholeness of that moment accessible. As the diverse facets of the picture become known, these individual perceptions constitute an ever more realistic and integrated image of the whole, and make new learning possible. The parts enrich the whole and the whole in turn gives deeper meaning to the parts. We discover an interconnecting coherence, a more fundamental reality that exists between singular perspectives, but does not become evident until these discrete truths are brought into a dynamic relationship with each other.

Surrendering Attachment to an Outcome

Surrendering attachment to an outcome means emptying out our expectations in favor of opening up to what lies beyond them. This practice is built upon the premise that our attachments and visions of outcome reflect our knowledge and experience of the past; they perpetuate a world that is known and predictable; and they protect us from a world that is not. These preconceptions reduce our capacity to respond to the call of the moment, to meet the truths of the present time, to learn. It is for this reason that detachment, the practice of non-attachment or emptiness, is emphasized as a universal spiritual discipline.

Practicing detachment is like voyaging into an unknown sea. Slipping one's moorings loose and setting sail for uncharted waters involves abandoning the safety of the familiar and sacrificing the comforts associated with old ways of knowing. When a learning community sets out together, it is a group of strangers with differing ideas about its destination and method for proceeding. These differing perspectives soon create tensions that manifest as chaos, alienation and competition for the helm. The temptation for the group (and frequently for the society) is to throw some passengers overboard and elect others as leaders.

What actually threatens the group's journey however, are the beliefs, prejudices, and preconceptions that have enabled the members of the group to come this far. The primary impediment the group faces is its own anxious desire to avoid relinquishing the safety of the known for the uncertainty of the unknown. The moment of real truth in a learning community comes when members begin to reveal the incompleteness and imperfection of their own knowledge. As they surrender their isolated realities constructed upon partial-truths, they begin to discover that, despite their pretenses of certitude, they have all along been sailing upon a sea of uncertainty.

This is a terrible liberation. Members find themselves exposed as uncertain, imperfect and incomplete beings; they experience a vivid sense of openness and existential vulnerability. Difficult as this experience can be, it holds within it a great solace, because this very vulnerability is the ground that humanity shares. Through practice, members build the strengths that allow them to be themselves and connect with others in the face of existential uncertainty. Standing upon this ground opens a new vista of self and world, their profound interrelatedness, and a compassionate awareness of the challenges inherent in being human.

Conclusion

As the twenty-first century unfolds, humanity stands crowded together at an evolutionary threshold. We are increasingly aware of the otherness of those who surround us. At the same time we are beginning to grasp how the political, cultural and ecological problems, that now threaten the survival of our species, cannot be adequately addressed without collaboration with them. It seems that we face a dilemma: in order to get along with the business of human existence we must learn how to get along with each other. Can we do it?

At the heart of this question lies a social koan. We face diversity, and must discover our underlying commonality. We are presented with threats to our survival, and must discover how to take our own positions without the righteous insistence about particular outcomes that inevitably threaten others' survival. Becoming responsible for a whole larger than ourselves, we must learn how to retain our own integrity without insisting that others forsake their integrity.

Gathering together to address these paradoxical tensions in a face-to-face learning community, we utilize the complications presented by our differences to deliver us to the place where our limited ways of knowing become evident. This is the threshold of an entirely different way of knowing. If we can find the courage to empty ourselves of certainty and open to a world of greater uncertainty, we gain access to a new mode of consciousness and a correspondingly more inclusive and complex sense of self.

When this occurs, group members re-discover the world and a new sense of the commons emerges. Personal well-being and the well-being of the whole are seen to be profoundly interrelated, both depending upon the quality of what we create between us. Access to this new, interdependent world is readily available to us. All we need do is turn toward each other and choose to learn what our differences have to teach us about the world we share in common.

From pages 213 to 222 of *Embracing Life: Toward A Psychology of Interdependence*, David "Lucky" Goff, Ph.D., Mill City Press, 2013

FACILITATION RESOURCES

Old age, especially an honored old age, has so great
an authority that this is of more value than all the
pleasures of youth.

—Cicero

Facilitation of Elder Groups

— Lucky

The assumption behind this document is that facilitation of any kind of group for elders must take into account the accomplishments of aging, the special characteristics of these folks. A group of individuals may have no idea these values are important to elders in general, but any effort to bring these people meaningfully together will be more successful if these values are considered when designing group-building activities.

Elder Characteristics

They are self-possessed and autonomous (responsible for themselves).

> They don't want or need anybody to direct them. They know when something is germane to them. They prize their freedom and opportunities for self-expression. They only need to know themselves better.

They are less emotionally reactive.

> They tend to be more capable of dealing with differences, emotionally-charged topics, and difficult realities. They have the ballast of what they know about themselves.

They are more capable of being interested, even intrigued by, differences.

> They tend to be more respectful and practice fewer efforts at domination. They seem to be capable of listening more empathically. The "other" is a gift that takes some diligence and creativity to unwrap.

They have a more compassionate outlook.

> They accept that pain and failure are necessary parts of life. They are thus able to relate to others who are experiencing these things. They also have a strong spiritual orientation that helps them put life difficulties into a broader context. They have some realization that their sense of self extends to others.

They are more relationally adept than ever.

> They do not like isolation, but enjoy solitude. They tend to communicate well (listening, as well as expressing), and have real empathy. They can stay with a difficult topic longer, if they choose to. They have some sense of what connecting socially takes.

They are egalitarian and concerned about everyone's participation.

> They are more likely to want to participate if they are in a social environment where freedom reigns. They tend to favor inclusiveness.

They have a spiritual orientation of their own.

> They have a variety of strongly-felt and idiosyncratic belief systems that help them find meaning as part of a larger whole. They are reasonably comfortable with death and their own lives. They are more tolerant and interested in the beliefs of others.

By and large they have a more complex awareness than the norm.

> They are more comfortable with paradox, learning, vulnerability and uncertainty. Because they know something of how connected they are, they tend to be happy, flexible and creative.

Facilitative Guidelines

1. Design all group activities with a special sensitivity to the autonomous and freedom-loving needs of elders.

2. Respect differences, and cultivate them.

3. Appreciate all flags (all ideologies) but don't let any of them dominate.

4. Infuse all activities with an ambiguously defined spirituality (in service to something larger).

5. Create various social opportunities (dyads, small groups and the group-as-a-whole).

6. Create a variety of opportunities for self-expression (play, talk, physical touch, movement, and other forms of creative expression).

7. Validate minority voices (underscore the message, courage and value of minority awareness).

8. Actively listen. Elders benefit by hearing themselves, but the facilitator might have to hear first. In any case, as facilitator one wants to stay close to the group without being captured by it. Be a reliable echo.

9. Encourage the personal and the transpersonal.

10. Affirm leadership as it emerges from the group.

Alignment

The assumption is that aligning personal focus on the part of the facilitative team, with the group's process, empowers both. It is definitely true that the facilitator's level of awareness opens the way for a group. The facilitators use their own awareness to exemplify possibilities. Facilitator growth and learning is likely (if fear doesn't dominate the group or the facilitators) to be available to encourage group growth and learning.

Group cohesion often parallels the cohesion of the facilitation (or hosting) team. Therefore, it is important that facilitation team members maintain an authentic relationship with each other. This means that all forms of relationship ups and downs can serve the unfolding level of intimacy in a group, if the facilitating team is willing to engage and learn. Angeles Arrien's "Four Fold Way" guidelines for interaction make that possible.

❧

Some Sample Elders Salon Agendas
2010 – 2013
—Alexandra

3/2010 First time –agenda is under "Getting Started" in main section, page 10.

4/2010

What do the terms "Elder Insurgency" and Rozak's "Longevity Revolution" evoke for you? Do you tie this in to the idea of Giving Back? Is creating a compassionate society part of this? What does that mean to you?

5/2010

What does "Making a Difference" or "Giving Back" mean to you? How can this group help you create more of a sense of purpose in your life? Support, action, as a sounding board, contemplation of current times or the future, creating subgroups for particular purposes, as a launching pad, OR?

6/2010

LOSS & NEEDS (their Gifts later)
Anticipation of the creation of a Caring Presence within the group; how do we create that, how can we be there for others?
What gifts have come from going through periods of Loss & Need? How have they made your life richer? What wisdom has been gained?

7/2010

WHAT ARE YOUR BIGGEST MONEY CONCERNS now or for older years? Do you have enough to see you through to 90 or 100?
If you still have living parents, is that becoming a financial or time issue? Are health issues a threat to your financial security?
If you're on Soc. Sec. with no retirement fund or pension, can you manage? Are you interested in time banking?

FYI   This was one of our least interesting or effective meetings.

8 & 9/2010

WHAT CHANGES HAVE MADE YOU WHO YOU NOW ARE?
Having only scratched the surface in August, we're diving more deeply into the subject of Change — to see what kinds of events shape us and bring us wisdom.

11/2010

HOW IS BEING ONESELF SUBVERSIVE? What is the difference between an Old Person and an Elder? Back to large circle to explore how being authentically ourselves is a radical or subversive (of current cultural attitudes) act.

1/2011

ELDERING AS SELF-INITIATION, Part I
HOW OLD ARE YOU NOW, AND WHEN DO YOU THINK YOU BECAME AN ELDER, if ever — or were willing to claim some degree of wisdom? When did you know you were no longer what you had been? What are the signs, the markers; what about it is important or distinctive? Is it still

going on? Our definition of elder: Did something die in the process? Are you willing to claim your wisdom? To be wise? Share your process.

2 /2011

ELDERING AS SELF-INITIATION, Part II
Shifting from responsibilities of the past to exploring present and future "response-abilities". It's an Inside Job.
The IN BETWEEN — the Quest, the Liminal.
How these cycles go on all the time in smaller or larger ways. The losses of health, friends, wealth and power make room for the unexpected.

This is where the self-confrontation, reclamation, and reformation occur. Discoveries come as gifts of loss, from forgotten areas of the self, values left behind, changes. In the In Between we can break down routine habits, grapple with the unfinished, face old fears, break with social conventions, and integrate innocence and wisdom. A reclamation of wonder and delight await!

3/2011

ELDERING AS SELF-INITIATION, Part III
1) What we, individually and collectively, as an Elder Generation want to hand on to those who follow.
2) What we've learned, pitfalls and successes; what we would still like to contribute, and insights from our experience.

4/2011

INTEGRATING ELDERHOOD:
So far in 2011 we have explored Self-Initiation and what we, individually and collectively as an Elder Generation, want to pass on. Has this been enabled and is further integration desired?

Dyads: If you feel integrated into Elderhood, what enabled you? If not, what do you need for completion? Initiation is a self-revealing process. Where are you in that? Ask yourself "How can I actively move ahead in this process?"

6/2011

PERSONAL STORIES about how our needs and desires for connection change as we age and about times when we have been well met in a connection. How has what I want from connection and relationship changed as I grow older? Have I wanted something more in/from my relationships? Stories of a profound moment of connection and what made it possible.

7/2011

WHAT WISDOM DOES THIS SUGGEST: "Take your well-disciplined strengths and stretch them between two opposing poles, because inside human beings is where God learns." —Rilke
The poles may suggest Paradox. What role does paradox play in the wisdom of Elders?

9/2011

AN EXPLORATION OF ELDER GRIEF, COMPASSION & PRAISE.
Grief is the Mother of Compassison. —Rumi
When you grieve the thing you lost, it means praise and when you praise the
thing you lost, it means grief! —Martin Prechtel
I saw that pain is part of beauty — that inside of all that music, all that love,
all the moonlight and sunlight, are shafts of pain, and we are meant to bear it
all. —Rebecca Wells

10/2011

Claiming Your Growing Elderhood;
Groups of 3-4: Who are the elders you've known and admired; what have
you learned about being an elder from them?
Come back to large circle – Claiming your growing Elderhood, what does it
mean to you?

11/2011

GENDER, NOW AND THEN:
Opening: Names & Call in a GENDER Trait to be present
Go-Round: Short expression of when gender issues were most problematic
in your life
FISHBOWLS: Spin bottle for men or women first. Use stories if you like
What are/have been the main experiences of gender/gender issues in your
lives? Two fishbowls – one men, one women. Switch to other gender.
Call back to big circle: WHAT DOES IT ALL MEAN TO US NOW?

12/2011

SOLSTICE & the TIPPING POINT:
Opening: Names. Light a candle with what you hope for in the new year:
personal, family, community, world OR toward pushing the Tipping Point
toward higher global (or other) consciousness
Big circle: What new initiatives will help us embody what we want in the
coming year? What do we elders have to bring to the Tipping Point?

1/2012

WINNOWING & ESSENTIALIZING:
Groups of 4: Weeding out or dropping activities - aspects of winnowing.
Paring down, becoming more efficient toward focusing on what really
matters.
Large circle – Essentializing: What IS becoming essential? This isn't because
you have to (energy), but because you want space for something that feels
important to come in – to help you occupy yourself. What does the sacrifice
from the winnowing make possible? You're giving up ... in order to have ...

3/2012

HOW OUR PERSONAL DILEMMAS CONNECT to the
PLANETARY DILEMMA: Opening: In a word or two, what is your first
reaction when confronted with a dilemma? One group of 4 or 5, fishbowl-
style, Lucky in to work with them to identify a growth-dilemma in each of
their lives.

Organize group into smaller groups of 4 to do the same
Large Circle to continue with the direction, and with last month's question
about what kind of consciousness is needed for growth, bigger dilemma and
personal dilemmas

4/2012

CAN PLAY SHIFT OUR DILEMMA?

Start to drum – pick up a rattle/drum & begin to move to the beat if you like
Dance & begin to play with & against each other
Acknowledge each other; let your feelings show
As you move, begin to make faces, let your imagination guide you
Know yourself and each other as part of the greater pattern, the web
Begin to notice the colors and shapes around you – find something brown
          and touch it with your left hand – for instance...
Something red and touch with the back of your right hand
Put an elbow on something in the purple family
Back up to something in a print
Touch your cheek to something blue
Put a knee up to something green
Shoulder to something grey
Etc,

Remember that we humans are animals — begin to mimic one of your choice
And another
Mimic one of your favorite endangered species
Begin to come to a quiet place – choose a partner and hold and feel each
          other's hands (Lucky will take us from here)

Dilemma Story read again
Large circle

5/2012

COMMUNITY — THE DIFFICULT SIDE

Open with intros and an honoring go-round
Small groups: Biggest pains received in community settings
Large circle: Biggest obstacle in yourself to joining with community

6/2012

WHAT ARE OUR OBSTACLES TO CONNECTING?

The honoring greeting of kissing the hands of others we meet while milling
Small groups with unnamed topic, possibly the kissing hands above
Large circle: Did you learn anything about yourself and the obstacles you
have in connecting with others?

7/2012

LIVING MORE SIMPLY

What you know about from your younger years that could be useful in case
of a general emergency, such as no fuel;
Reducing carbon footprint;

Are there characteristics of our Elder Culture that are holdovers from what we learned in the 60's and 70's?

8/2012

RELATIONSHIP — WITH OTHER - I
Intro/names / Who has been your most important relationship — name & relationship (mother, brother, husband, wife, friend, teacher) no story

The Fragile Bond - Dyads: What has this (important relationship) and relationship in general taught you?

Bring back to large circle: What do you want NOW from your
        relationships?
How is what you want and how you "do" relationships different now?
How is the way you relate to yourself and to others the same/different now?

9/2012

MORE RELATIONSHIP — WITH OTHER, DEEPER IN - II
Intro: My name is ...; the longest gap between my intimate relationships is ...

Dyads: Mirrors – Looking at self and owning attitudes – other-defined and self-defined

How has your relationship ability changed?
What do you want NOW from your relationships?
Do you still have the same patterns or have you grown?
How is the way you relate to yourself and others the same or different now?

10/2012

RELATIONSHIP WITH OTHER - III
Milling exercise (eye gazing?)
Large circle for duration: Relating to difference

11/2012

IN THE SOUP & EMERGING: Are we "younger" now?
Ask new people to introduce themselves, they point to one person to do the same. Rest of us say our names. If no new, we all pull faces at each other and group, no names (OR, we point to someone, then they point to someone until everyone is in)

Four small groups. Gor tells the story of the chrysalis or cocoon (we call it "soup" or goo because the caterpillar turns into a goo and comes out transfigured)
Talk about personal experiences with the soup
Large circle: Reflect as moved

12/2012

A version of last December agenda – candle ritual.

1/2013

About here we stopped writing up agendas because we began to have more or less regular ways of doing things, the agendas were sufficiently simple, and we were sufficiently confident to not do so.

LEADERSHIP

To exist is to change, to change is to mature,
to mature means to go on creating oneself endlessly.
— *Henri Bergson*

Leadership:
Serving the Unfolding Whole
— Lucky

Introduction

With the change in the paradigmatic assumptions of our age, there is a corresponding change in the role of leadership. Where once vision and the ability to persuade and inspire others were seen as the essential components of leadership, now a new way of envisioning leadership is emerging. Not surprisingly, leadership is now seen more fluidly as a role that takes on many forms. In this discussion I will be focusing primarily upon the role leadership plays in facilitating the unfolding of community life, increasing a group's functionality. I will identify key leadership sensibilities and describe how these sensibilities may be acquired.

Leadership Is a Group Role

Arnold Mindell made an important contribution to how group leadership is perceived when he pointed out that leadership is a "group role." By this he means that the leader is a group construct, a role that arises in order to serve the unfolding needs of the group. Mindell has gone on to point out that leadership has a transpersonal dimension; that is, the role of leader and the function it serves is greater than the personal capacities of any individual. No one person can long fulfill the demands a group places upon the leadership role.

What Mindell is pointing out is that the role of leadership is a group archetype, much like the scapegoat/messiah archetype described by Arthur Colman. This role is a manifestation of the unconscious of the group and a means by which the contents of the unconscious can be brought to consciousness. Understanding leadership's relationship with the group's unconscious is a prerequisite to serving well in the role of leader.

The unconscious dimension of the leadership role can cause many problems in group and community life. One of the primary problems it causes is confusion about leadership itself. For instance, in order for a group to achieve its highest functional capacity, the role of leadership must be able to move around. That is, the unconscious of the group must have the capacity to select the forms of leadership that are needed in order to facilitate the next stage in the group's development.

Community life, then, is frequently accompanied by struggles around leadership. Assigned or pre-selected leaders may find themselves suffering a variety of leadership challenges from members of the group. These challenges can be seen as desirable or undesirable, threatening or unthreatening. How leadership challenges are viewed will be determined by three factors: the leaders' development, their experiential knowledge, and their ability to buffer anxiety. First, does the leader have a solid and well enough differentiated sense of self to be able to continue functioning while being challenged. Second, does he or she have experience with the role the unconscious plays in unfolding community life. And third, does the leader have the ability to buffer the anxiety of the group and help the group welcome leadership when it emerges.

When a group's assigned leader (and/or its members) know that the unconscious of the group is trying to express its wholeness and developmental desire through raising up new forms of leadership, it is a lot easier to embrace and make use of these forms of leadership. Without that knowledge these challenges may be viewed suspiciously and the formal leader of the group or the group's members may thwart the group's development by trying to eliminate these challenges.

Leadership as a group role poses another interesting and challenging problem for group members. Anyone in the group may be drafted into a leadership role by the group's unconscious. Group leadership is not always voluntary! You may be selected to serve the group's development because you hold a particular awareness or sensitivity. You may or may not be comfortable with being thrust into a leadership role. When it happens, you will become the focus of the group's attention, and you may very well find your actions scrutinized by group members who are critical of what you represent. This is an anxiety-provoking experience. Your ability to hold onto yourself and to represent the awareness or value of your sensitivity may well determine to what degree the group will learn and grow.

Key Leadership Sensibilities

Group leadership, as you have now seen, can take two different forms. It can be explicit, taking the form of a pre-agreed upon, consciously selected leader. Or it can be implicit, arising as needed in an informal, unconscious way. This latter form of leadership may not be agreed upon by anyone, least of all the person (or persons) drafted into the role. And, often, these two manifestations of leadership may well collide, creating conflict and confusion in a group.

No matter what form leadership may take, its primary function is to increase awareness in the group. Thus leadership involves introducing a group to unknown aspects of reality. This includes helping a group handle its emotional reactions to an emerging picture of reality that may be disturbing and destabilizing. Then a leader may be called upon to help a group discover how to integrate into itself this new reality. In order to fulfill this function a group leader needs to have sufficiently acquired some of the following capabilities. Leaders must be capable of the following:

- Holding wholeness (maintaining a systemic perspective)
- Embracing complexity
- Buffering personal and social anxiety
- Tolerating and sustaining dialectical tensions
- Taking things personally and transpersonally
- Serving when drafted

Let's look quickly at each of these capabilities and how they serve to increase group awareness. Then we will also look at how these capabilities can be acquired by those who wish to hone their leadership skills.

Holding Wholeness

The primary asset a good group leader relies upon is his or her capacity for holding wholeness. This capability is not based upon a conceptual framework. Learning systems theory will not give you the ability to hold wholeness. Instead, this capacity is born out of lived experience. It is the product of long immersion in the dynamic life of social organisms. As one gets acclimated into the tensions that abide in all social relationships, connections become visible. These connections eventually reveal the larger workings of the system as a whole. When one is directly in contact with these living processes then the concepts introduced by systems thinking become experientially meaningful. They enable a leader to view the workings of the whole operating in the details of the moment. This viewpoint can be brought to the group's experience to aid the group in acquiring a recognition of its own wholeness as it unfolds.

Embracing Complexity

As we have shown elsewhere, groups evolve through opening themselves and including new forms of awareness and experiences. For this kind of growth to occur a group must have the capacity to embrace a world that is more complex than imagined. Thus a leader needs to have the ability to step into the turbulence that always exists at the edges of the group's consciousness. A group leader must pay attention to the discrepancies of group life. He or she must be willing to disturb the group by pointing out the places where the group's words, actions, and values are not aligned. By pointing out discrepancies, and the unknown processes and beliefs that account for them, a leader introduces the group to a larger, more complex reality. This is how a group comes to know its own wholeness.

Buffering Personal and Social Anxiety

Groups seldom welcome new awareness, especially if it appears to threaten group stability or precious assumptions. Strong emotions can be aroused. These emotional reactions create anxiety. So a leader must be capable of withstanding the group's reactions. This means he or she must be able buffer their own anxiety. They must be capable of taking a differentiated position vis-a-vis the group, one that affirms diversity and stays engaged. To the degree a leader can handle their own anxiety, then they can also serve the group by helping to buffer the group's anxiety. A non-reactive leader can help a group endure the rollercoaster ride of emotional reactivity. As the leader inquires into, and reflects upon, the group's reactivity, he or she assists the group by bringing awareness to its struggle with what it doesn't know or doesn't want to know.

Tolerating and Sustaining Dialectical Tensions

The leader's ability to buffer anxiety also serves as an essential leavening agent that facilitates group development. Earlier we pointed out that group life is defined by unresolvable tensions. Immature groups try to resolve these tensions. To grow a group, then, needs a leader (or leaders) who are capable of tolerating more tension than the group can handle while affirming the value of these tensions. This form of leadership serves the unfolding wholeness of the group by affirming the group's latent ability to handle these tensions. But early in the life of a group this leadership function will not be very welcome. The leader may become the focal point for resentment, hostility and hatred. This challenges the leader's maturity and discloses the group members' possibilities. If a leader can handle it, then group members have reason to believe they themselves will be able to find the way.

Taking Things Personally and Transpersonally

One of the great ironies of leadership is that the leader must eventually die. The role of leadership must move around. Thus a leader must be willing to empty himself of his attachment to being the leader. This sacrifice imbues the group with responsibility for leadership and affirms the group's capacity to assume this responsibility. And the refusal to make this sacrifice thwarts the group's development. Thus a leader must be willing to take his or her role transpersonally, as something that goes beyond him or herself. By transcending the role, the leader becomes part of a larger leadership function, one that draws upon the accumulated wisdom and maturity of the whole group. In this way the community assumes responsibility for the organization and re-organization of its own consciousness, a significant step toward maturity.

But taking things transpersonally is not all a leader must do. A leader must also be capable of taking things personally. He or she must be willing to submit to the constant scrutiny and feedback of the group's members. A leader must take the group's feedback personally to look at what it reveals about his or her limitations, biases, and unconsciousness. A group relies upon the leadership function to help it become more conscious and adaptable. If the group is going to acquire the capacity to constantly update the accuracy and acceptability of its own self-image, then it needs leadership that embodies this capability. The rigor this imposes upon the leader is great. A leader who will take things personally, and not simply as projection, models this skill for the group as a whole, and increases the effectiveness with which the leader serves the group.

Serving When Drafted

How you serve when you are drafted into the leadership role will likely determine how you feel about the prospect of leadership. The call to leadership is not always an explicit one. But it is inevitable. Suddenly you find yourself exposed, the object of attention, the one in the headlights. You will be scrutinized and judged by the group. This is through no fault of your own, nor of the group's. You cannot avoid it; all you can do is decide how you will respond to it when it comes.

If you do not see yourself as a leader, and you have no desire to undergo the rigors associated with leadership, this experience is going to be highly anxiety-provoking. You may feel like you are being made the identified problem of the group or a project the group has decided to work on. If you don't want to be traumatized by this experience, you will need to learn how to take it personally *and* transpersonally. It is no accident that you have been chosen. You embody some quality of awareness or sensitivity that is now essential to the group's well-being. You can help yourself if you take this personally. Use the group's attention and feedback to learn more about yourself and the quality you hold.

You can also help the group if you refuse to only take it personally. You also represent something significant about the group's unconscious, something that is trying to come to consciousness through the group's focus upon you. You represent an aspect of the group's wholeness that it may or may not want to deal with. If you can stand up for what you represent and affirm the value you hold for the whole, you may be able to help the group transform its consciousness. In the process you will be learning more about what the leadership role asks of all of us.

Acquiring Leadership Sensibilities

The aforementioned leadership sensibilities are not simply skills that one acquires through study and practice. They are sensibilities that arise with the emergence of a more complex and inclusive form of consciousness. Acquiring the ability to exercise these capabilities means undergoing a process of repeated transformation. You may believe you understand the conceptual framework from which a particular sensibility arises, such as systems theory, but that understanding isn't enough by itself to enable you to hold wholeness or embrace the complexity of chaos. These capabilities are acquired through experience.

Not only must you undergo immersion in the fire of experience but, if you want to enhance your capacity for leadership, you must do it with others. For others are truly your teachers. In addition to exposing you to a world beyond your experience, they will introduce you to your own unknown self. Others will hold you accountable for your choices and the impacts they have. In this way they will hone your awareness and enlarge your worldview. To acquire the capacity to lead there is no real substitute for immersion in community life.

When you extend your circle of caring far enough out into the world, you become vulnerable; the world enters your life more fully. Community life will empty you of your preconceptions, it will reveal the offensiveness of your defenses, and it will ask you to embrace vulnerability. Ultimately, community life will ask you to develop your ability to connect deeply with others while remaining true to yourself.

In the final analysis, community life will teach you that leadership emanates not from what you know, but who you are.

Annotated Bibliography for the above on Leadership

Greenleaf, Robert, (1970), *The Servant Leader*, published by the Center for Applied Studies, Cambridge, MA

> This brief pamphlet sets out Robert Greenleaf's groundbreaking leadership ethos. Greenleaf lays out his awareness that, more basic than the systems, ideologies, and movements (that do not make themselves but are made by individuals) that generate the massive problems of our times, is the incremental thrust of an individual who has the ability to serve and lead. His second concern is for the individual "who tends to deny wholeness and creative fulfillment by failing to lead when he or she could lead."

Greenleaf, Robert K., (1998), *The Power of Servant Leadership,* essays by Robert Greenleaf edited by Larry Spears, published by Berrett-Koehler Publishers Inc., San Francisco, CA

> This is a collection of eight of Greenleaf's most compelling essays offering his best insights into the nature and practice of servant-leadership. Servant-leadership emphasizes an emerging approach to leadership which puts serving others and community first.

Jaworski, Joseph, (1998), *Synchronicity: The Inner Path of Leadership,* Berrett-Koehler Publishers Inc., San Francisco, CA

> This is a book that guides the reader through the process of one man's development of essential leadership capabilities. Written from the heart as well as the head, this book describes Jaworski's discovery of the deep issues of leadership. Here he offers a new definition of leadership and illustrates how one releases human possibilities and breaks free of organizational and self-imposed limits.

Palmer, Parker J., (1998), *The Courage to Teach: Exploring the Inner Landscape of the Teacher's Life,* Jossey-Bass, San Francisco, CA

> Parker Palmer is a master teacher and a man who has lived in intentional community most of his life. In this book, which ostensibly focuses upon the inner landscape of a teacher's life, he reveals the leadership dimensions associated with learning in community. In so doing he reveals a fundamental premise: good teaching (like good leadership) cannot be reduced to a technique; good teaching comes from the identity and integrity of the teacher.

Wheatley, Margaret J., (1992) *Leadership and the New Science: Learning about Organization from an Orderly Universe*, Berrett-Koehler, Inc., SF

As a leader in the field of organizational transformation, Margaret Wheatley has integrated the latest developments in a shifting scientific paradigm to redefine the leadership role. Here she describes how the principles that underlie quantum reality, chaos, and complexity theory all offer insight into new ways of leading organizational and social change.

From pages 384–392, *Embracing Life: Toward A Psychology of Interdependence*, David "Lucky" Goff, Ph.D., Mill City Press, 2013

The Minority Voice

— Lucky

This awareness, about the minority position, first came to me from Arnold Mindell. I don't know what he is doing with it now, but I have a sense it could be valuable to us as elders-in-training, and to the community that is coming through us.

Our elder community has been exploring what I have come to think of as a budding elder characteristic — that is, an ability to be intrigued by the *other*. I think our sense of community is grown by our fascination with our differences. The learning that I value so much, seems to emanate from our diversity not our similarity. So, I feel moved to go further in exploring the phenomena of differing.

Sometimes in differing one is made, or becomes, the other. This is a good thing that has happened, but almost all of us know something about how painful and off-putting this can be. The scrutiny of others, particularly a group of disturbed others, is hard to take. Being one among many is not easy. It takes all the maturity one has to hold onto oneself and to withstand the machinations of a group trying to digest something it is having a hard time with. History is filled with the bad things that a majority can, and does, do to a minority. This is a moment rich with possibility that is always hard won.

Minority awareness always advances awareness, but it isn't always welcome. Being someone who holds some kind of minority awareness in our families, communities, or culture is an important role (for the whole) that isn't easily fulfilled. The larger system, family, community, or culture, may need new awareness, but they seldom easily accept it; and the first messengers of that awareness are not often treated all that well. So, it is important in a differentiating world to know something about taking care of oneself when occupying the minority position.

The minority position is inevitable in a world where our uniqueness is to be included. Eventually everybody is a minority of one. This is how complexly our world is constructed. Strangely, each of us also bears gifts for the whole. Giving those gifts, however, can be a challenge. To do so well means withstanding the rigors of being in the minority position for the sake of all involved — self and social system. This is a complex maneuver, which we elders are learning about and are probably more capable of than those with less life experience. It's good because we are probably going to need all that life experience to hold onto ourselves and actually offer an alternative. That, I believe, is part of the service we budding elders can offer.

Like it or not, we are going to occupy the minority position, so let's occupy it to the best of our ability. I don't necessarily know all that that means. I am learning from our experience together, but I do have a few ideas.

1) Expect to occupy the minority position
2) Learn how to hold onto (take care of) yourself
3) Serve the whole (try to deliver the awareness you hold for everyone). Know the whole is depending on you.
4) Be thankful this kind of learning has finally come your way.

I am writing primarily about items 1– 3. Expecting to be in the minority position and to hold some kind of awareness for the whole, is what is going to advance our learning together and our impact in the world. We feed each other when we practice community together, but we also challenge each other. To connect deeply, to be able to give our gifts to each other, we also have to get better at holding onto (taking care) of ourselves. This is a highly idiosyncratic experience, one we are all depending upon each other to do. The strength of our bonds depend upon it, and we force each other along the way when anybody occupies the minority position well enough to rattle our cages.

There is a great paradox that resides at the heart of community — one that strengthens us but also asks us each to go beyond ourselves. To be connected deeply to others, we have to be deeply connected with ourselves.

This is what I have to offer: this process of our being together, becoming more important to each other, is the real teacher here. I'm just glad I get to go for the ride.

৵

COMMUNITY

*Genuine community starts with the realization
that reality isn't psychological.*

— Martin Buber

*Because we have forgotten our kinship with the land,
our kinship with each other has become pale.
We shy away from accountability and involvement.
We choose to be occupied,
which is quite different from being engaged.
In America, time is money.
In Kenya, time is relationship.
We look at investments differently.*

*—Wangari Waigwa-Stone
(born & raised in Kenya)*

Why Community?

— Lucky

Community is humanity's natural social habitat. The evolution of human sentience is deeply intertwined with thousands of years of life within small bands. It is fair to say that what makes *homo sapiens* human emerged from the results of years of interactions within a group and still more years of the group's interactions with the natural world. Community, therefore, has traditionally served as the social context which mediated relations between members of the band and between the band and larger cosmos.

In today's modern world our sense of community is largely lost, having given way to the alienation and social ennui that has resulted from the fragmentation and massification of modern society. But, the human need for community has not subsided despite the disruptions of mass society. Now more than ever we suffer from the loss of connection and belonging that community provides. And, even more poignantly, we suffer from the loss of the capabilities that participation in community engenders in us.

We have not selected community as the primary focal point for our inquiry into group work merely out of sentimentality for what has been largely lost, nor out of an effort to preserve what may be an endangered social organism, although these are worthy objectives. We will focus our attention upon this context because community best provides the requisite depth of social complexity we need to shed light on all the larger and smaller levels of group experience.

As we will soon see the circle of community embraces and includes the intrapsychic realm, the interpersonal, the group, the cultural and the global (including the more-than-human community). This complexity makes community an ideal context for learning about ourselves, each other, and the way our interactions in group create, perpetuate, or transform cultural tendencies which then impact upon all of us (and our environment).

There is yet another more transpersonal reason we view community as the optimal context for exploring group work. Community is the action domain where the contents of the social brain, our collective consciousness, can be made explicit and reflected upon. Community thus offers us the opportunity to observe the social dimension of the transpersonal at work, and thereby provides an opportunity to practice group mindfulness.

All of this potential is enfolded into the experience of community. For the true transformational value of community comes with immersion in the interactive flows that comprise the life-blood of a community. This handbook is thus intended to provide you a variety of perspectives that you can draw down upon to make your experiences with community more meaningful. You may also find new concepts that will guide you towards new behavioral options so that you can extend your repertoire of meaningful ways to connect with yourself and others.

Finally, life in an on-going community provides several important ingredients that are essential for the process of human evolution, be it at the individual level or the cultural level. On the individual level as social creatures we rely upon those we interact with for our own development to provide us with a special blend of support and challenge. We need to be seen and recognized for who we are, to feel known and like we belong. This supports our process of becoming ourselves. We also need to be held accountable for the impacts that we make upon others, so that we can learn how to function as a member in a larger social organism. We also need the challenges that come from contact with others who perceive us, or reality, differently than we do. This introduces us to a more complex reality than we had previously apprehended and enables us to integrate ourselves more fully into the larger world in which we are embedded.

When most people think about community they envision something like the vision of community described by John Winthrop, on the Mayflower as the pilgrims were about to step foot into the new world.

> For this end we must knit ourselves together in this work as one person; we must entertain each other in brotherly and sisterly affection; we must be willing to

abridge ourselves of our superfluities for the supply of others' necessities; we must delight in each other, make others' conditions our own; rejoice together, mourne together, labor and suffer together, always having before our eyes our community as members of the same body. In so doing we will see much more of divine wisdom, power, goodness, and truth than formerly we have been acquainted with.

—*John Winthrop, 1630*

Such is the exacting nature of community that the process a group must go through to actualize the ability to "delight in each other" and "make others' conditions our own" involves experiencing another facet of community. As Father Jean Vanier, the founder of the L'Arche community in France describes it, this aspect of community life can be described as a terrible place.

> Community is a terrible place. It is the place where our limitations and our egoism are revealed. It is the place where we discover our poverty and weaknesses, our inability to get on with people, our mental and emotional blocks, our affective or sexual disturbances, our seemingly insatiable desires, our frustrations and jealousies, our hatred and our wish to destroy. While we were alone, we could believe we loved everyone. Now that we are with others, we realize how incapable we are of loving, how much we deny life to others.
>
> So community life brings a painful revelation of our limitations, weaknesses, and darkness; the unexpected discovery of the monsters within us is hard to accept. The immediate reaction is to try to destroy the monsters, or to hide them away again, pretending they don't exist, or to flee from community life and relationships with others, or to find that the monsters are theirs, not ours. But if we accept that the monsters are there, we can let them out and learn to tame them. That is growth toward liberation.
> — *Father Jean Vanier, Community and Growth: Our Pilgrimage Together*

We have seen in the last century the collective monsters that can be unleashed upon the world when human beings refuse to take personal responsibility for their "limitations, weaknesses, and darkness." Community is the terrible place where we discover these monsters and it is the place of grace where these monsters can be tamed and we can discover more of "divine wisdom, power, goodness, and truth than formerly we have been acquainted with."

As we shall see through a combination of interacting and reflecting together, community can become a form of social crucible, an incubator that provides the combination of support and challenge necessary to stimulate the development of new consciousness. Community also provides us the social context, the social practice field, wherein we can apply our new consciousness and develop new behavioral options. The process of building such a community will ask much of us. If we are willing and able to rise to the occasion, then the community we create together offers us the opportunity to participate in the processes of social evolution by which we as a species will insure our own future.

Pages 315–318, *Embracing Life: Toward A Psychology of Interdependence*, David "Lucky" Goff, Ph.D., Mill City Press, 2013

Community Growth

— *Lucky*

Introduction

Entering into the 21st century we find ourselves inhabiting a natural and social environment unlike any our ancestors have known. Through our own successes we have transformed our world. Once we occupied a world full of dangerous mysteries. The animal powers held sway, and humankind huddled together in small bands. Now our numbers, restless energy, and creative curiosity have overcome the animal powers and unlocked many of Nature's secrets. Through our own success we now find ourselves crowded together on a rapidly shrinking planet, occupying a landscape that is increasingly man-made and thoroughly dominated by the activities of our own kind.

There are many uncertainties that attend this moment in our species' journey. We enter this century unsure of our future — not in the same way that our ancestors were insecure because they felt so small in such a large and mysterious world. Instead, when we look out upon our world, we are confronted by a distressingly familiar danger: we ourselves have become the most dangerous mystery we face.

Our journey has brought us to a point where we must confront our own kind. For it is evident that our technological virtuosity, having delivered us to an age of incredible possibilities, now threatens us (and the living systems we depend upon) because our social development, our ability to relate to our own kind, has not kept pace. This is the nature of our current evolutionary dilemma. To ensure a future worth living, we must find the way to embrace the complexity of our own humanity.

And where, other than our interactions with others, do we have the opportunity to do this? This study guide will focus your attention upon the benefits and the challenges inherent in the social dimension of being human. It will do this by focusing primarily upon what happens when humans interact in groups. In so doing you will be challenged to look at your own relations with others through the many social contexts you participate in. Your attention will be directed toward the common dynamics that unfold in groups. If you understand these dynamics and have the developmental wherewithal to respond to them, this understanding can be used to increase the quality of your connection with others. As you will discover, the intention of this path is not only to make it possible for you to interact comfortably in groups, but also to help you discover how your participation in groups can be turned toward the benefit of all.

Defining Group Work

Groups are ubiquitous in human life for we, as a species, are social animals. Early in our lives we are utterly dependent upon the group we call our family for our survival. This group itself, if it is to supply the nourishment and protection needed by our young, depends upon the functioning of larger groups such as the extended family, the church, school, or local community. These groups in turn rely upon even larger, more complex groups in order to function well. Thus human life is immersed in level upon level of group activity.

You have no doubt participated in many types of groups dedicated to child-rearing, learning, accomplishing tasks, making decisions, making money, healing, spiritual development, creating social change, or protecting our natural environment. No doubt you have also participated in groups that functioned well and those that barely functioned at all, groups that were inclusive and those that were exclusive, groups that felt safe and warm and those that felt dangerous.

Most likely your experience in groups has done more to teach you what it means to be human than any other experiences you have had. Group life has shaped how you perceive and respond to other human beings. Group life has also shaped what you believe to be possible between human beings (for better or for worse).

As Charles Cooley, one of the early founders of sociology, made clear early in the last century, the group is the place where not only the self is born, but also where the other is first experienced. As this study handbook will show, groups are the places that both necessitate and support the further evolution of one's sense of self and one's ability to relate to the other.

Community then, as we define it, involves inquiring into how the group context functions best to support an evolving relationship between self and other. Toward that end we will focus upon a single group context: community. We look at how a group becomes a community, how the sense of community is sustained as it evolves, and at how community serves as an incubator for the evolution of consciousness and the transformation of self-other relations.

Awakening Together in Community

This section of the handbook will devote attention to the typical dynamics that unfold in any social organism, be it a family, work group, church or nation. By examining the processes through which a community comes into being, stabilizes itself, develops a communal identity, protects or surrenders that identity, learns and evolves, we will be observing the same dynamic processes that shape group life wherever it occurs and at whatever level in human society.

You will be aided in this inquiry by your experience as a member of the social organisms in which you are a part — particularly by the experience you will be sharing as members of a social organism in the process of evolving. In this way you will be taking an integral approach to community, looking at the surface descriptions of community provided by the literature while simultaneously exploring the internal dimensions of the experience as they manifests in your thoughts, emotional reactions, and interactions. Let's begin this phase of our inquiry by looking at how a group of individuals creates an experience of community.

Defining Community

Anthropologists note that the characteristics that distinguish *homo sapiens* from our earlier hominid ancestors — tool-making, language, and meaning-making — arose as a result of social interactions. They emerged as attributes of the social brain. Despite the agreement that community played an instrumental role in the emergence of the species, anthropologists and sociologists alike have a very difficult time defining community.

This inability to agree upon a specific and enduring definition of community has been an ongoing source of confusion, one that will likely emerge during the course of our interactions with one another. This confusion about defining community reflects the multi-dimensional nature of community. Both the phenomenon and the experience of community are multi-leveled. One's experience of community unfolds over time and, as it does so, new dimensions of the experience reveal themselves. Similarly, community as a living organism unfolds over time revealing new, unanticipated qualities. Thus, at any given moment one's experience of community is defined by two central factors: the consciousness of the particular observer and the current developmental level of the community being observed.

As you endeavor to create an experience of community among yourselves, while reflecting upon the nature of community together, you are going to be like the proverbial blind men examining the elephant. Each of you will bring your particular consciousness to different features of the overall experience. Like the blind men, each of you will "know" your experience describes community. And like the moral of the tale of the blindmen's encounter with the elephant, you will soon find that it is only through sharing your differing experiences of community that you can begin to grasp more of the wholeness of true community.

The Community-Building Process

The process of building community involves learning how to bring together all of the capabilities, beliefs, limitations, judgments, prejudices, sensibilities, and strengths of a group of strangers, so that all of this wealth of perception, experience, and meaning-making can be available for the benefit of all. This is a complex task, one that reflects the same level of challenge that we as a species are struggling with now as we endeavor to create for the first time a global sense of community. To accomplish this we must approach it like enlightened blind men, simultaneously holding to our own experience of wholeness, opening to the experiences of others so we can see a greater wholeness beyond.

M. Scott Peck describes a four-stage process of how the experience of community emerges. This pattern reveals how a social organism, as a holon, evolves. Just like each of us, a group must transcend its parts and include them in a larger, more complex whole. Community relies upon and requires the distinctiveness of its members to propel its own differentiation. At the same time community relies upon our burgeoning capacity to open ourselves to each other, and requires us to embrace the more complex reality we introduce to each other for its own integrative processes.

Let's look more closely at how a group manifests community and how that community then goes on to evolve the depth and breadth of an extraordinary group. Peck's model shows that a group of strangers will at first emphasize their similarities and tend to conform to a basic level of politeness that forestalls any awareness of their differences. Such a group is undifferentiated. The group's emotional processes will pull for mutual-validation and sameness. This is comforting to the part of you and part of the group that seeks to belong, but arouses anxiety for the part of you and part of the group that wants to manifest your distinctiveness and exercise your autonomy.

The group will at first become anxious about, and try to minimize, differences. If the anxiety about differences in the group is sufficient, it will not tolerate differing and it will quickly marginalize and exclude anyone who reveals too much distinctiveness. A group that succeeds at this may look very coherent and cohesive on the surface, but the intersubjective experience of "we" that such a group will produce will be very narrowly defined, rigid, and highly brittle. If, however, the group contains enough individuals who have the capacity to regulate their own anxiety — that is, who are not too reliant upon external-validation for their sense of wellbeing — then they will begin to reveal their distinctiveness despite the social anxiety in the group.

When this happens, the "chaos" phase of the community-building process begins. In this phase of development a group struggles with an escalating competition between distinct ideas about how the group members should interact and toward what end. In this phase the diversity in the group is starting to manifest. And as it does, even more personal and social anxiety is aroused. It is during this stage in a group's life that members begin to joust with one another trying to create, often in a well-intentioned way, their own version of community. In essence the group will be struggling to determine "whose form of community" the group will adopt. Since there are many different forms of community being offered, the selection of any one will result in the exclusion of others. This usually threatens some members' sense of belonging.

This is often a painful and anxiety-provoking moment in a nascent community's life. As Peck points out, many groups will seek to return to the politeness and comfort of pseudo-community rather than endure the social anxiety and uncertainty that chaos brings. If a group succeeds in returning to this earlier stage, it does so by foreclosing upon its chances of becoming a true community. What happens here is critical. There are two ways to go forward, and each has a price. One way leads back to politeness but at the expense of a chance for true community. Groups will select a leader, find an outside enemy, look for a scapegoat or a subgroup to blame, or organize themselves in some other way. Each of these actions is intended to reduce the group's anxiety by eliminating the tensions aroused by diversity. And each of these actions will eliminate any possibility that the group will be able to create a real sense of community.

By viewing the group as a social holon we can see what is really at stake for the life of this organism. If the group is to avoid self-dissolution, dissolving into a jumble of smaller parts, and maintain the possibility of self-transcendence, attaining a larger more complex unity, it must find a way to make its parts distinct whilst integrating them into a more coherent whole. Efforts to organize will only lead to self-dissolution (and the exclusion of some members of the group). Most groups fail to move beyond this point.

The genius of Peck's model is the recognition of a way through this dilemma via self-transcendence. When the members of the group realize the futility associated with the ongoing struggle for the preeminence of their viewpoints and then step up to the realization that all of their viewpoints are partial and inaccurate, the group has a chance of reaching community. Peck called this phase of the community-building process "emptying."

Emptying involves surrendering the beliefs, judgments, prejudices and assumptions that you hold onto to secure your worldview and the sense of self you have built upon your version of reality. Emptying means walking out into the world naked, undefended by the precious beliefs that you have held onto to protect yourself from uncertainty and vulnerability. When a sufficient number of a group's members are willing to empty themselves, they create an atmosphere of openness in the group that is inherently inclusive and receptive. From this shared experience of existential vulnerability, an experience that all humans have in common, there arises a new sense of community.

When the parts of a social organism are willing to go beyond themselves, the whole social organism transcends itself and becomes a larger, more integrated being. It is this movement that transforms the intersubjective experience of "we-ness" that underlies true community. When it occurs, the social organism reorganizes its consciousness and its identity, thus enabling its parts to interact in new and more meaningful ways.

Concluding this discussion of the community-building process, I want to point out that the community-building process is essentially a description of the way a group transforms its own consciousness. The social holon evolves in the same essential way that an individual does — by opening itself to a larger, more encompassing reality. In the next section you will turn your attention to the way that a group sustains an ongoing sense of community. It turns out that learning is essential to the process of maintaining and expanding community.

Annotated Bibliography

Gozdz, Kazimierz, (1995), *Community Building: Renewing Spirit & Learning in Business,* New Leaders Press, San Francisco, CA

> This is a compilation of articles that describe how community building can transform the workplace and generate greater cohesion and meaning within corporate life. The book is organized around the central vision that corporate life provides a venue wherein community can take root. This is a treasure trove

of approaches to building and nurturing community in a variety of business settings. It is full of pragmatic approaches.

Peck, M. Scott, (1993), *A World Waiting To Be Born: Civility Rediscovered,* Bantam Books, New York, NY.

> In this sequel to *A Different Drum*, M. Scott Peck describes the way civility is undermined and narcissism supported by the fragmenting forces of mass society. By focusing attention upon the loss of community, Peck underscores the things that ail us as a people. He also points out to us how our social potential is being squandered as well as how it can be restored.

Sustaining Community

Community is not simple or straightforward. Community arises because individual members are willing to undergo the rigors associated with emptying themselves. When a group achieves an experience of community, it naturally wants to protect and maintain it. Sustaining a sense of community turns out to be a rather paradoxical enterprise. For the more a group tries to hold onto the sense of community it has achieved, the more it imperils community. Let's look at how this occurs.

Community, like all developing organisms, evolves in a stage-by-stage process. Most organisms are instinctively programmed by nature to undergo metamorphosis at the appropriate time in their life cycle. But humans and the social organisms we form have to deal with another order of complexity to evolve. We have to transform our consciousness. This means that we have to undergo willingly the ambivalent experience of surrender. For an individual human being to evolve he or she must be willing to surrender the self they have for the sake of the self they want to become.

Similarly, a social organism must be willing to surrender the sense of community it has established for the community it wants to become. It is for this reason that some community builders say that the greatest obstacle to community is community. The hard-won sense of community must be given up or it will rapidly evolve into a newer, more complex form of pseudo-community. Improvement that it might be, this new form of pseudo-community will nevertheless represent only a portion of community's potential because it embraces only a part of the larger reality in which it is embedded.

From this vantage point you can see that the community-building process must repeat itself if a sense of true community is to be sustained and maintained. The vitality and integrity of community life depends upon ever-renewing cycles of community-building. Each cycle means emptying itself of the old sense of community in favor of opening up to a newly emergent experience, each time sacrificing the ground it is built upon to open itself to the unknown.

No community can long sustain itself and transform its consciousness into a more encompassing and inclusive form without placing an important emphasis upon learning. Learning is an essential skill that all social organisms must embody. Your next set of readings will elaborate upon this point. We will return to the significant role learning plays later when we describe integral collective practices designed to enhance group consciousness.

Dynamic Tensions in Community Life

A human community is a living organism. It has a life cycle of its own and is subject to the same kind of dynamic tensions that all living systems must contend with. As a social entity it is constantly challenged to balance the needs of its constituent parts with the needs of the whole organism. A community's survival and the vitality of the life it leads depends upon how it handles tension. In this section we will take a look at some of the normal tensions that are inherent in all living systems, tensions between structure and chaos, stability and change, inclusion and exclusion, and togetherness (unity) and autonomy (diversity). Let's look at how these irreconcilable tensions shape community life.

Structure and Chaos

You have already seen that a community's growth and development are determined to a large extent by how it handles the tension between structure and chaos, between form and formlessness. Every form of human social organism must acquire some basic structural features. A social organism will have to feed, house, educate, protect, and regulate its members. To do so it will evolve norms of behavior and differentiated roles. Because a human community is sentient, it must also evolve an additional level of structural requirement, which is consciousness. This structure arises through language and the ability to make shared meaning, out of which a community derives a value system, a worldview, a culture, and a sense of identity.

As you saw during our discussion of how a community sustains itself, these necessary and often hard-won, structural features serve to perpetuate a sense of community. Paradoxically, if they are clung to too tightly, they can also threaten the vitality and adaptability of community. Here we run into another facet of nature's design that is very highly disturbing to community life. To sustain itself and increase its adaptive functionality a community must be able to tolerate chaos. In fact developmental system theorists have shown that sustained systemic transformation, the ability to periodically forgo one community structure for a larger more inclusive one, is only possible when a system has the ability to tolerate operating near a chaotic threshold. (Ford & Lerner, 1992.)

The intersubjective experience of balancing these tensions can be quite disturbing to community life. In any given instance members may feel themselves compelled to advocate for order to ensure continuity and maintain comfort or to work to undermine structures that feel oppressive and limiting. Frequently, these tensions will manifest in the form of conflict between members (or subgroups). Without awareness of the normality and appropriateness of these tensions, these conflicts can be perceived as merely personality conflicts between individuals. And, as we shall stress repeatedly throughout this discussion, groups will frequently try to avoid or solve these tensions through a variety of mechanisms that isolate, marginalize, and exclude members.

Stability and Change
Community as a social organism also faces the challenge of balancing the need for stability with the necessity for change. Stability enables a

group the opportunity to integrate its various parts into a more cohesive and coherent whole. Stability enhances a group's ability to function; it enables predictable patterns of behavior, which then support the members in orienting themselves to the emerging group culture. Stability allows the members of the group to grow close to each other, to gain familiarity and rely upon each other.

The closeness that stability supports, however, can also become stifling. Closeness and predictability, if taken too far, can lead to pressure for conformity and sameness. The pressure for stability then threatens autonomy and the individuation processes of the group's members. These processes, in turn, threaten stability because they introduce disturbing new forms of behavior and innovative ideas. So while stability permits a group to adopt the structure that is necessary to enable itself to function well and meet its members needs, it is change that stimulates growth and a higher order of adaptation to reality, which in turn is necessary to meet other needs.

The intersubjective experience of these tensions can manifest in members who feel compelled to organize the group around stabilizing processes designed to minimize the rate of change for the sake of feelings of connection, security, and safety. When these essential needs are threatened, these members will find the prospect of change anxiety-provoking. On the other hand, other members may find themselves trying to organize the group around processes of change designed to undermine oppressive or coercive patterns. These members will consider themselves advocates for essential needs such as openness, autonomy, individuality, and freedom. When these needs are threatened, these members will find an emphasis upon stability anxiety-provoking. As with all of the tensions we are describing here, groups will find them disturbing and may try to minimize or eliminate them by ostracizing, attacking, or eliminating members who offend the prevailing mood of the group. And as you shall soon see, as social organisms, groups are frequently disturbed and upset by the normal and appropriate, unconscious, self-balancing attributes of living systems.

Inclusion and Exclusion

As a community forms, it takes on a shape of its own, an identity. The process of identity formation is one that involves balancing the tension between what is included in the group's emerging sense of identity and what is excluded — between what is considered "us" and what is considered "not us."

A community cannot function well if it doesn't assert and maintain a boundary. Without this boundary no one will know if they belong or not, nor will they know how to participate. Thus the exclusive nature of boundary formation is essential to the emergence of a community identity and all of the subsequent processes that ensure the integrity of a given community. These same processes define the nature of what is included in a community's consciousness and what is relegated to a community's unconscious.

Naturally, the very same processes that ensure the emergence of identity and consciousness, when held too tightly, diminish the health and functionality of a community. The urge to protect a hard-won sense of group identity and shared consciousness leads to the refusal to incorporate awareness and information that might upset the status quo. Thus exclusiveness can harden and become oppressive. This limits the ability of a community to adapt to changing life conditions and learn. And the refusal to adapt endangers the long-term viability of the community.

The intersubjective experience of these tensions can manifest in members who feel compelled to protect the group's hard won identity by refusing to admit new members, by asserting the primacy of group needs over individual needs, or by making sure that group norms of communication and behavior are always followed. These members are defending the need that we all have to feel like we belong in something larger than ourselves. Other members may feel compelled to challenge the prevailing norms, will seek to introduce innovation and advocate for greater openness to new members and new experiences. These members are also working on behalf of the need to extend membership to include more of life's experiences.

Community identity is as essential an ingredient to community life as individual identity is to a human life. No community can function very well for long without some sense of identity. Similarly, no community can long endure if it isn't capable of surrendering and transforming its identity. A community cannot survive if it isn't capable of being exclusive. Nor can it survive long if it isn't capable of surrendering exclusivity long enough to transcend itself and include more of reality. This means that community life is beset with ongoing skirmishes around inclusion and exclusion. When efforts are made to eliminate or solve these tensions, through the organizational patterns that groups employ to relieve chaos, communities endanger themselves and their members' well-being.

Togetherness and Autonomy

As a result of nature's design specifications, community life is governed by the twin urges for autonomy and togetherness, for diversity and unity. These twin pulls generate tensions that can arise intrapsychically, interpersonally, in intra-group interactions, and between the group and the larger culture it is embedded in. Individual members will feel anxiety about how much their sense of self is identified with the group. Depending where they are in their own development, members may have a compelling need to deepen their identification with the group or to differentiate and reduce their identification. This means group members will be constantly struggling to balance these tensions as they interact with each other.

In the meantime the community itself will experience being pulled by these same tensions. In order to fulfill its desire to belong, a group will seek to enforce group norms that are consistent with the larger culture. In order to fulfill its desire for autonomy and wholeness such a group will seek to enforce practices that enhance diversity and that counter the prevailing norms of the larger culture. Community life, therefore, ensures that there will be a lot of social anxiety around togetherness and autonomy.

The group will be constantly engaged in the process of balancing its internal tensions, which arise as members interact, with its external tensions as the group interacts with its environment. These tensions generate high stakes for individual members and for the group as a whole. How well a community and its members handle these tensions will likely determine how cohesive the group is, as well as how adaptive the group can be.

A Reminder

Let us remember that one of the characteristics that defines life is tension. The tensions that govern the life of community are natural. They are irreconcilable tensions. Communities and their members sometimes believe that their inability to resolve the conflicts that these tensions generate means that there is something wrong with individual members or with the community itself. This is not the case. These tensions are not resolvable; as uncomfortable as they make community life for a community's members, they also ensure the vitality of that life.

Some comfort can be taken from the awareness that community life is beset with unresolvable tensions. For once one adapts to this awareness, these tensions then become a catalyst for learning, for growth and development. In the next section you will see how these tensions and the anxieties they produce generate the emotional life of a social organism. You will also learn how a community can begin to observe its own emotional processes.

Emotional Process in Community

A community, like an individual, is always engaged in a struggle to maintain a dynamic ever-shifting balance. A human community, however, has a task that is somewhat more difficult than the one faced by the individual. For the constituent parts of a community are conscious. Its members experience ambivalence about suffering with these tensions. This experience is by-and-large an emotional one. For a community to grow and develop, its members must be willing to suffer the emotional strains that occur as the community struggles for balance.

With a human community the willingness to take on this suffering is never assured. This is what can prevent the "terrible place" that community can be from becoming the place where we "delight in each other" and "make others' conditions our own." No individual or group starts out knowing how to handle these tensions (and the suffering they generate). The process of acquiring this skill also involves suffering. At first one must be confronted by more tension than one can handle, so that one can learn to handle more. This feels like suffering that is being imposed upon us. Later, when you have gained in maturity, you can choose to suffer the necessary losses that are required for personal or community development. But in order to do so you must first learn how important and meaningful this kind of suffering is.

In this section you will look at the underlying emotional processes that emerge as a community and its members struggle with these dynamic tensions and the suffering they generate. You will be introduced to four patterns of response to these tensions that play themselves out in all social interactions, be they interpersonal, inter-group, or intercultural. By examining these patterns you will develop a greater awareness of how we as a species create more suffering than is necessary because we are not willing to suffer the necessary suffering that these tensions impose upon us. This discussion should assist you with identifying the patterned ways you respond to these tensions in your life. This awareness could help you discover how you can reduce the suffering you experience, as well as to become more at choice about the suffering you help perpetuate as you interact with others.

As you have already begun to see, you (and communities) suffer because of a tendency to manage your relations with others so as to reduce the threat of a more accurate picture than you can accept. This suffering is largely neurotic and unproductive. When a group sustains its identity in this way, it ends up creating systemic forms of suffering. There are three typical patterns of response to the natural tensions of community life — dominate, submit, and distance — which attempt to manage these tensions so as to minimize impact upon the accuracy and acceptability of the group's identity. Let's look at how these patterns create and sustain suffering while shaping community life.

Dominate

Dominance essentially means you try to exclude or eliminate the other's reality. This involves asserting the pre-eminence of your reality. Diminishing others' realities is a way of preserving the illusion that there is only one view of reality (or what is right). Dominance is designed to obliterate differences so as to avoid the experience of vulnerability and existential uncertainty that arises when the accuracy of one's self-image or worldview is placed in doubt. This attempt to minimize the tension of diversity feeds and reflects cultural dynamics such as political correctness, fundamentalism, ideological imperialism, and ethnic cleansing.

Managing tension through this pattern can look and sound like: over-functioning, having "the answer," or knowing what's best for someone else; defensively arguing or taking affront when challenged; sulking or punishing when you don't get your way; taking the moral high ground; feeling reassured (superior) because someone else has problems or inadequacies; feeling threatened because someone else doesn't have the problems you have (worrying about inferiority).

Your preoccupation with coercion and comparison (doing it or having it done to you) has to do with the theme of domination. Because the underlying premise of domination is that there is one (dominant) reality, if you don't make your reality "the reality," then someone else will make you sign on to theirs. Unpleasant as this either/or situation is (and the fighting and bickering that manifest from it), this stance nevertheless holds the unspoken notion that reality is singular and there is a right answer, somewhere. This is seemingly less anxiety arousing than grappling with the fact of multiple realities and the uncertainties and contradictions this awareness generates.

Examples of dominance include physical violence, oppression, judgmentalism, assuming superiority. This can also include canceling out the other's reality with supposedly "well-intentioned" gestures like rescuing, over-sympathizing, or sentimentalizing differences away as sometimes happens when people insist that "We're all one" or "We're just human."

Submit

Submitting means excluding your own reality or point of view. The essential stance of submitting is to join the reality of the other. This involves abandoning oneself and excluding the validity of one's own reality in an effort to avoid the uncertainty and vulnerability that come with a real, close examination of one's own worldview and the self-image that is built upon it. Managing tension through this pattern can look and sound like: under-functioning; compliance; underestimating oneself; choosing to not choose; living by an external standard; e.g., "following the rules," or "being a good _____."

To avoid too much anxiety, individuality is traded off for togetherness. As difficult as it is to give up oneself in this way, what is evidently more aversive is the experience of being in conflict with others and facing the reality of choice and responsibility for one's life. This pattern is akin to animals that take a submissive position to reduce challenge and gain acceptance into the pack.

Examples of submission include: unawareness, silence, and adopting the ways, thoughts, and values of the other, blaming oneself instead of confronting others (or the situation), appeasing instead of challenging. Polarizations in relationships, groups, and cultures are a complementary process of dominance and submission. These emotionally reactive processes feed cultural dynamics such as internalized racism and sexism as well as the segregation and marginalization of those who lack social rank — ethnic minorities, the old and disabled, children, etc.

Distance

Distancing involves attempting to exclude the relationship with self and thereby between self and other. In this pattern an effort is made to avoid experiencing oneself, either by internal psychological processes or by avoiding emotional interactions that would trigger internal experience. Similarly, this pattern attempts to reduce social anxiety by pretending that no social connection exists or that it isn't important if it does. This strategy props up a false sense of self-mastery by avoiding the vulnerability and the existential uncertainties aroused by direct experience with otherness.

Managing tension through this pattern can look and sound like: denial of feelings, values, abilities (emotional cut-off); being confused, forgetful or obscure as a way of disowning oneself; a whole continuum of being "out of touch" with oneself, including substance abuse, dissociation and psychosis. The central attitude of distancing is to treat others (and more deeply, to also treat oneself) as a thing or an object. Rather than being oneself and experiencing one's life, there is a sense of using or controlling oneself. Although there is a clear disrespect and devaluing of self (and of any significant relationship with another) in this stance, it is apparently better than the two other choices: facing up to not being able to control others or facing up to genuinely knowing and mastering oneself.

This pattern occurs on the cultural-political level in the following forms: the self-marginalization of militia groups, cults, and isolationistic national policies. This also includes maintaining the ability to remain untouched by the suffering of others who are "on the other side" of the street, check point, de-militarized zone, or world.

Differentiate

To differentiate, in the context of this discussion, means to maintain your own reality while engaging openly with the reality of the other. This means knowing your values and experiences, expressing them frankly, and owning your own position. At the same time, it means inquiring respectfully into the experience and perspective of the other and allowing it to touch you, to be included in your increasingly complex (even contradictory) understanding of reality. In other words, you are being who you are because it is important to you to do so, and not because you are compelled by someone else, and not in order to compel or control someone else.

Managing tension through this pattern means deliberately working to acquire the ability to tolerate tension in order to embrace a social reality that is more complex than was imagined. This response is predicated on the awareness that some forms of tension are useful and important, such as the anxiety and tension inherent in growing. This contrasts with the way the other patterns view tension — as stressful but not productive. Those attempts to avoid tension lead to neurotic suffering.

A differentiated response to the tensions that are part of community life involves taking one's position (discerning and expressing one's reality)
- For one's own sake
- Without manipulating or trying to change others
- Without attachment to a particular or preferred outcome.

The touchstone of differentiation is being honest with yourself; i.e., being willing to go through whatever you have to go through to maintain an accurate and acceptable sense of self. In other words, differentiating means realizing that who you are and how you engage in the world is completely up to you. Differentiating can look and sound like knowing what you want, feel, think, and won't do; distinguishing between needs and wants; requesting what you want and living with the responses (or non-responses) you get from others; saying honest yes's and no's; sharing experiences and ideas but not requiring that they be important or useful for anyone else; differing with important other people. It is only the ability to hold onto oneself and to stay non-reactive in the presence of another that makes genuine contact and real intimacy with a world beyond one's own.

After reviewing these patterns, we can see that the fourth pattern — differentiating — is self-focused: stability arises from defining oneself, a dynamic process of maturing into "more" of who one is. This response enables us to embrace these tensions, accept the necessary suffering that comes along with them, and grow ourselves by updating the accuracy and acceptability of our self-image. This choice promotes a sense of internal security and a sense that one's well-being rests within oneself. When a sufficient percentage of a group's members are capable of this last form of response, there will also arise a sense of internal security and wellbeing within the group. Such a group is acquiring the capacity to learn and is on the way toward becoming an extraordinary group.

It is important to emphasize how sharply this contrasts with the first three patterns that are all other-focused; that is, they attempt to maintain psychological stability by manipulating the relationship with others. It is these patterns that make a group dangerous. A group's refusal to undergo the necessary suffering associated with acquiring a more accurate and acceptable self-image leads a group to focus its attention upon the individuals or subgroups which attempt to bring new awareness to the group. Such a group will employ whatever relationship tactics it feels are necessary to avoid suffering self-doubt and anxiety. In the process a group will try to shift this suffering to others. The next bibliography will focus upon this aspect of group life, one that reveals the contents of the group's unconscious and begins to point toward the way to arouse and awaken the group's collective consciousness.

The Group Unconscious

What I have been describing thus far is the way an emerging experience of "we" arises; that is, how a group of individuals becomes a community, and beyond that, how a community grows and evolves itself. I have also described a variety of challenges that a community faces along the way. For a group to grow and transform its own nature, I have shown that it must develop a capacity for surrender. You have looked at the equanimity-disturbing process of trying to balance irreconcilable tensions and seen how a group's responses to these tensions and its willingness to suffer will define its emotional system and the types of interactions it is capable of. You are now poised to begin examining another important developmental challenge — that is, the way a group begins to become aware of itself and develops consciousness.

In the early stages of community life, there is very little self-awareness in a group. Many of the processes we have been exploring operate beneath the consciousness of the group. Thus it is necessary to focus attention upon the unconscious processes of the group in order to begin to observe and make them palpable. To focus attention upon the unconscious of the group, however, requires a distinct shift in one's perceptual field, one that requires us to move our attention beyond our individual struggles to the experience of the group as a whole.

If you know what to look for, the group's unconscious becomes visible. I have already noted how tension reveals the self-organizing activities of the group's consciousness. By observing the group's use of language and metaphor, one can get a sense of the concerns that are operating beneath consciousness. Relationship processes and conflicts are indicative of the group's struggle to maintain or shift a precarious balance. A group's members will manifest a host of physical sensations such as stomach tension, shallow breathing, sleepiness, tight muscles and emotional volatility. All of these sensations can be used to get a grasp on the group's unconscious emotional processes. Group members will have dreams that can be considered "group dreams." The figures that appear in these dreams and the scenarios that get played out can all disclose additional information about what operates at the edges of the group's consciousness.

The relationship a group forms with its unconscious will likely define just how functional and adaptive a group will become. Typically most groups have no awareness of unconscious processes and are therefore run by those processes. Sometimes the group's emotional processes will not impede the group in performing its functions, and this lack of awareness is not very problematic. But groups that need to be able to function at high levels are going to be impeded and their functionality limited unless they are developing some capacity to observe and respond to the contents of the group's unconscious. This is also true for communities, social organizations, nations and civilizations.

A community that hopes to mature and stabilize itself enough so that it can learn to function as a complex adaptive system must have access to the wealth of creative intelligence that operates beneath consciousness. This intelligence, because it is unconscious, manifests at first through non-rational processes. Thus a group must be prepared to sense and tolerate things that make no sense. Observing these non-rational processes — such as emotional outbursts, uncontrolled movements, periods of hysterical laughter, daydreams, jokes that won't go away, and difficulty starting or ending meetings — a group begins to gain access to another way of knowing.

Unconscious processes can be very powerful. They can contain primitive energies (the monsters) that feed upon fear and anxiety. They also harbor transpersonal energies that can transform a group's consciousness. Sometimes these energies can be identical. Learning to work with the unconscious, then, is when a group learns to hold, observe, and learn from non-rational processes. Groups fail to hold these non-rational processes when they insist that they make sense. A group has to overcome its discomfort with the unknown so that non-rational forms of intelligence can introduce the group to aspects of reality that have to be experienced before they can be understood.

For a community to evolve itself and actualize its social potential it must develop a repertoire of ways of observing and responding to its unconscious. Your next reading suggestions will introduce you to one particular method for gaining access to the unconscious and bringing its contents to awareness. This method, known as dialogue, offers a group an attentional practice that, when practiced diligently, can generate a form of group mindfulness. Along the way this practice can also begin to make palpable the experience of participating in a collective form of consciousness.

Dialogue is one form of collective integral practice. Before you are done exploring the intersubjective realm, I will introduce you to several more. I want to focus upon dialogue now because it offers an important perspective. Dialogue reveals to us that a community is a microcosm of the larger social/cultural surround in which it is embedded. When a community begins to examine its own unconsciousness, it is also beginning to disclose the collective consciousness of the species. This is a significant development. When a community discovers that it is a microcosm of the larger surround, it also discovers that it can begin to work on global issues locally through the members' interactions with each other. As an awakened social holon, a community has the ability to increase the integrity and consciousness of the larger social surround. Such a community furthers the evolutionary process of our species by merely working with the contents of the collective unconscious as they manifest in the community's life. In the next section let's look at how this is so.

Annotated Bibliography (for section above)

Colman, Arthuur. D., M.D., (1995) *Up from Scapegoating, Awakening Consciousness in Groups,* Chiron Publications,Wilmette, IL

> In this book Arthur Colman, a Jungian analyst, describes the role that the Messiah/Scapegoat archetype plays in the unconscious life of a group. He uses a combination of myth, storytelling and group experiences to describe how groups can bring to consciousness the contents of their own collective unconscious. In doing so he provides vivid descriptions that can assist group leaders and members in the process of working with the powerful forces inherent in the collective unconscious.

De Mare, Patrick, (1991), *Koinonia: From Hate, Through Dialogue, to Culture in the Large Group*, Karnac Books, London, UK

> In this study of the group, particular attention is paid to the processes and dynamics whereby the group micro-culture emerges. This occurs as the initial frustrations of the group find their expression through hate, and as hate initiates and is transformed by dialogue, and as dialogue ultimately establishes what the Greeks knew as Koinonia, the state of impersonal fellowship. This book demonstrates how a larger group, by the very nature of its size, offers a structure and a medium for linking the inner world with the cultural context.

Mindell, Arnold, Ph.D., (1995), *Sitting in the Fire: Large Group Transformation Using Conflict and Diversity,* Lao-Tse Press, Portland, OR

> Arnold Mindell is one of the world's most gifted group facilitators and transpersonal theorists. In this book he shows how attention to power, rank, revenge, privilege and abuse can help build lively and sustainable communities. He demonstrates how the non-rational aspects of community life frequently signal the operations of the group's unconscious. He specializes in drawing attention to, and deconstructing the unconscious power dynamics that operate in all social organizations. Finally, he illustrates throughout this work how to stay centered while sitting in the fire of conflict and diversity.

Wolff-Salin, Mary, (1988), *The Shadow Side of Community and the Growth of the Self,* CrossRoad Books, New York, NY.

> A psychotherapist and member of a religious order takes a close look at what it means to live in community, whether it be a religious community, a family, or a primary relationship. Using case material from her own experience, she sheds light on the shadow side of community life — the effects of power, anger, fear, and withdrawal — and goes on to show how, out of the elements of pain and conflict, individuals in community can achieve greater integration and growth of the self and the community itself can become more life-affirming.

❦

Awakening the Social Mind

Our exploration of community has, until this point, focused upon how a community comes into being and develops sustainability. These are the prerequisites for the emergence of a community identity. You have also looked at the dynamic processes that define the identity and functionality of a community. Community, just like an individual, expands its ability to function through the transformation of its consciousness. A mature community will undergo a number of such transformations. As you will now see, this is a prerequisite for becoming an extraordinary community, the kind of group that can support both individual and cultural transformation.

To become such an extraordinary community a group must develop an ability to tolerate transformation; it must, in the language of systems thinkers, learn how to function near chaos. This, too, is an acquired skill. Acquiring this skill requires disciplined effort. Just as an individual needs the support of a spiritual practice to achieve the farthest reaches of human development, a group needs collective practices to achieve extraordinary capabilities. In this section we will bring to your attention several collective integral practices — that is, group learning methodologies that are employed to awaken and transform collective consciousness. After introducing you to the essential ingredients of these practices, I will go on to describe how they awaken the social mind.

Let's start by looking at what comprises an integral practice. Ken Wilber describes such a practice as one that "exercises body, mind, soul and spirit in self, culture, and nature." He goes on to add that "the more categories engaged, the more effective" the practice will become. (Wilber, 2000, *Integral Psychology*, pg. 114.) This tells us that for a practice to be truly integral it must have the breadth to encompass the "I," the "We," and the "It," as well as the depth to embrace multiple levels, from the body to the spirit. A collective integral practice then must also address and encompass a similar breadth and depth of experience. Here again we can turn to the words of Ken Wilber: " a truly 'integral transformative practice' would give considerable weight to the importance of relationships, community, culture, and intersubjective factors in general, not merely as a realm of application of spiritual insight, but as a means of transformation." (Wilber, *A Theory of Everything*, pg. 54, 2000)

You have already been exposed to dialogue and M. Scott Peck's community-building practice. Now let's consider the attributes these practices share and employ to transform consciousness. When practiced together, these disciplines encourage the emergence of a more complex form of awareness by bringing consciousness to the collective unconscious, thereby awakening the social mind. Let's look at each of these disciplines more closely.

- Experiential learning
- Focused attention
- Inclusivity
- Multidimensional (systems) thinking

- Personal responsibility
- Shared reflection
- Detachment
- Ecological awareness

Experiential Learning

Group learning requires us to risk and expose ourselves as we engage with each other. Learning always involves a risk of self. Without risking, neither you nor your group will acquire the capacity to tolerate anxiety, a hallmark of maturity, for the sake of a more accurate and acceptable picture of self and social reality.

Each of these practices engages us in a form of action-science, whereby we conduct a series of interactive experiments. These experiments reveal the underlying hypotheses (assumptions) we live by. The interactive responses they generate provide feedback which makes our assumptions more visible. Through action we expose ourselves to feedback that will provide data that confirms, contradicts, or points our discrepancies between the assumptions we operate on and the reality they encounter.

These practices, by virtue of their reliance upon experiential rigor, arouse awareness of the resilient and adaptive nature of the self. They support the acquisition of the ability to maintain contact with oneself and the other in the midst of anxiety-provoking interactions. With sufficient practice they reveal the individual self (and the self of the community) to be a dynamic unfolding process. This revelation emerges through the benefits of shared observation and reflection upon the results of many such experiments.

Personal Responsibility

Group learning practices in general place a strong emphasis upon personal responsibility. These approaches view personal responsibility as having two essential vectors. An individual is simultaneously responsible for his own experience and well-being and for the experience and well-being of the group. Viewing personal responsibility in this way reflects a basic understanding of the holonic nature of the individual. The personal integrity and wholeness of the individual is essential. Equally essential is the individual's ability to participate in, contribute to, and identify with the wellbeing of a larger social organism.

Due to the dual nature of personal responsibility, this discipline places an emphasis upon skillful communication. The individual is encouraged and supported in taking responsibility for him or herself and is offered practices that encourage skillful ways of communicating personal truth. These are intended to assist individuals in retaining their own shape and holding their own positions. This helps members engage more fully and maximizes the diversity available in the group.

At the same time these approaches offer practices that focus attention upon how we interact, practices designed to bring consciousness to the complexity of social reality, making more palpable the multi-faceted nature of truth. These practices support a dialogue between "enlightened blind men" in order to help piece together a more accurate and complete picture of reality. In the process they arouse awareness and increase consciousness of the complexities and rigors of social interdependence. And finally, when practiced in conjunction with the other disciplines described herein, they reveal the depth inherent in community life and support the development of forms of consciousness that embrace that depth.

Focused Attention

Attentional practices represent another hallmark of collective integral practices. Each of these approaches provides practices that focus attention to enhance awareness and facilitate learning. These practices enhance integral awareness because they focus upon I, we, and it. "I" is examined by focusing attention upon identifying, examining and suspending our assumptions, judgments, and agendas. "We" is examined by adding inquiry into the perspective of others. And "It" is examined by shared inquiry into the context from which our assumptions emerge and the processes by which we assign meaning to them.

These attentional practices highlight the usefulness and limitations of mental models. They reveal how attachment to our assumptions distorts perception and separates us from direct experiences. They generate an extended field of awareness. They increase interest in, and tolerance of, contradiction, ambiguity and paradox. They help develop, when practiced with shared reflection, a multi-perspectival awareness and facilitate the emergence of group consciousness.

Shared Reflection

Group learning methodologies become integral practices when they emphasize shared reflection. By shared reflection we are here talking about practices that help a group's members begin to examine together the judgments, assumptions, perceptions, conflicts, and vulnerabilities that attention has brought to awareness. These practices invariably involve explicitly naming these assumptions and working together to inquire more deeply into their roots, the meanings they hold, and the impacts they generate. This enables a group to free itself from being held captive by unconscious assumptions. A group that develops a capacity to "hold" assumptions and reflect upon them becomes more choiceful. It acquires a greater capacity to regulate itself and is less prone to be run by the contents of its unconscious.

Shared reflective practices support the emergence of complex and multi-leveled perceptions. They allow patterns and inter-relationships to become visible. They support the emergence of synergies that further extend group awareness, and they render more palpable the underlying interconnectedness of the group's experience.

Inclusivity

An essential discipline for all groups that want to learn and develop consciousness, is the practice of inclusivity. For learning inherently involves addressing the unknown and taking it in. Thus, these practices involve paying close attention to the tendency toward exclusion, whether it takes the form of exclusion of self, others, or relationship. This practice involves identifying and observing processes that are intended to invalidate or dismiss the reality of others.

These practices essentially focus attention upon patterns of denial; they then encourage inquiry into these patterns and what they are intended to deny. By promoting awareness of patterns of denial these practices extend the awareness of the group toward its edges. This engages the group's unconscious and brings unconscious processes closer to awareness. These practices support the emergence of minority positions and the differing forms of awareness they embody. Ultimately, they enable a group to acquire a greater capacity for the openness that is necessary for genuine learning.

Detachment (Surrender)

Perhaps the most integral of the group learning disciplines is detachment, for it is this discipline that enables a group to surrender and transform its consciousness. A group that cannot tolerate undergoing the death-like experience of re-organizing its consciousness will not adapt and grow, nor will it support the growth and development of its members. This discipline is there as a lynch-pin which determines the transformative potential of all of the other disciplines.

Practicing detachment is difficult, for it involves much more than simply staying detached. Practicing detachment asks us to notice our attachments and to get attached enough to them to really grasp how significant they are to us. Thus practicing detachment asks us to identify and inquire deeply into what matters most to us. In order to practice detachment, we have to care enough to really be attached, for we cannot really surrender what we are not fully attached to.

The virtue of this practice is directly related to the preciousness of what we surrender. This is not a passive practice. It requires us to actively sacrifice the ground upon which our sense of self has been built. This ground is found in the assumptions we hold about the nature of reality, about our own make-up, about what is sacred. Giving up our ideological positions means surrendering the stances we take to protect us from uncertainty, meaninglessness, and awareness of how incomplete and vulnerable we actually are.

Practicing detachment then helps us acquire a capacity to live with uncertainty and vulnerability. This practice facilitates a fluidity of consciousness, a radical form of openness based upon not-knowing. When a group practices detachment it acquires the ability to live "near chaos" and to reorganize its consciousness fluidly. This opens a group's consciousness to the full breadth and depth of community life. Practicing detachment enables the group to consciously participate in its own evolution.

Multidimensional Thinking

The discipline of multidimensional thinking develops our ability to perceive wholeness. It helps us to see the relationship between different orders of reality, such as the relationship between the pain in my stomach and the decision-making process presently occurring in the group. Essentially, multidimensional thinking makes connections between different levels of experience. In this way it is identical to what others call "systems thinking." This form of thinking, however, is not restricted to an abstract analysis of something that lives outside of one's experience. Rather, multidimensional thinking involves us in the process of making sense of the complexity of our lived experiences by making connections with the context we are immersed in.

Paying close attention to dialectical tensions (such as tensions between stability and change or togetherness and autonomy) is one practice that supports multidimensional thinking. Another important practice involves looking for patterns that prevail across many levels. These "isomorphic" patterns reveal connections between what goes on inside the individual and what goes on at the cultural level. An example of an isomorphic pattern is systemic racism. Systemic racism is the cultural expression of the prejudices and projections of millions of individuals. It is also the perpetuation of prejudice through cultural processes that reinforce biases and unconsciousness.

The discipline of multidimensional thinking helps us see how our personal choices create or reinforce cultural dynamics that can have global impacts. It also reveals the way larger cultural processes, such as advertising, shape our beliefs. Finally, the discipline of multidimensional thinking makes it possible for us to recognize how our connection to these larger processes can be experienced through our personal emotional responses. Thus we discover the suffering of the rain forest manifests in an individual's despair, or that a community's unconscious desire for greater freedom of expression can catalyze a member's emotional outbursts. This discipline helps us to make palpable the web of interconnections that underlie our experiences and reveals the actions of spirit in each unfolding moment in a community's life.

Ecological Awareness

Another integrative feature of group learning is the way that it cultivates ecological awareness, an awareness of the implicit unity of all experience. This form of awareness is visceral and sensuous. It extends the sensory apparatus to include the felt sensations and lived experiences of the larger organism of the human and more-than-human community.

Ecological awareness arises out of the synergies that are created by the combination of disciplined practices we have thus far described. By practicing together we begin to create a form of group mindfulness that is capable of not only reflecting upon the contents of consciousness but of a more direct experience of reality. Practices that cultivate ecological awareness enable a community to experientially grasp the reality that all choices have social and environmental consequences. These practices sensitize a group to these connections, thereby increasing the likelihood of more socially and ecologically responsible choices. Ecological awareness also enables a group to align itself with the larger forces of life, to live in greater harmony with these forces, and to draw upon them for support and meaning.

To conclude this section we return to the following assertion: group work offers us the only viable method for acquiring the latent social capabilities that reside in the collective unconscious. Group work provides us with a means for unlocking this innate social potential and awakening the social brain. As a community evolves, it will necessarily have to reorganize its consciousness in a step-by-step fashion. Each step increases awareness and raises consciousness.

Consider this as you interact. Every time you inquire into your own assumptions or reflect upon the assumptions you hear being expressed in the group, you are making the processes of the group mind more explicit. Each time you stretch yourself to include something that seems unknown and "other," you are increasing the complexity of the group's mind. Each time you surrender a preconception that separates you from the truth of the moment, you are opening the group's mind to the larger reality that exists beyond all assumptions. In the following way you will learn of a variety of practices that can assist you in gaining access to a larger, more complex form of consciousness. Adopting any of these practices will assist you in making sense of your experience. So, too, will it assist the group in gaining access to the workings of the social brain.

Finally we offer this important reminder: you are engaging in a challenging and exacting process, one designed by nature for nature's purposes. To gain the benefits nature offers, you must be willing to step up to her requirements. And her requirements will transform how you see yourself. We conclude this with the words of Martin Buber who describes this journey and the transformation it evokes.

> All living with the whole being means danger; there is no thing, relation, or event in the world that does not reveal an abyss when it is known, and all thinking threatens to shatter the stability of the thinker. He who lives his life in genuine, realizing that knowledge must perpetually begin anew, perpetually risks all; and

therefore his truth is not having but becoming."

—Martin Buber, *Between Man and Man*

Summary

In this section I have endeavored to provide you with a number of ways of viewing the experiences you are having in the communities of which you are a part. By looking at how community is created and later sustained I have provided you with a description of how groups evolve. All along the way I have emphasized the many ways that groups, as social holons, are like individuals (only more complex).

By describing the correspondence between the patterns of individual development and group development I have shown you how your own lived experiences can be employed to understand group life. I have also tried to demonstrate how group life can help you see your own lived experiences in new ways. As you have examined the irreconcilable tensions that govern group life, the unconscious means groups employ to manage these tensions, the emotional reactivity they generate, I expect that you will be seeing your own internal life mirrored in the life of the group. For in fact, you are a composite being struggling to create a sense of community amongst your constituent parts.

As our discussion of the nature of group life has shown, there are patterns of interaction that repeat at all levels of human experience. I have described patterns that are intended to minimize diversity in order to preserve unity. I have also described patterns that maximize diversity in order to establish a higher order of unity. These patterns operate within each one of us and within the groups of which we are a part. As you shall soon see, these patterns reflect the evolutionary process. I have concluded this section by focusing upon group learning practices that awaken the social brain and give us access to the broader scope of collective consciousness. My intent is to help you recognize that your ability to actualize your personal potential is intimately interwoven with our species' ability to manifest its social potential.

Lest we fear that actualizing these potentials is beyond our individual and collective means, we will now turn to a discussion of the role that sociability has played in the evolutionary process. By examining the way spirit manifests in the life of nature we can see our natural endowment. We can take heart from the realization that we can draw down upon the creativity, strength, and resilience of the processes of evolution. And better yet, learning from them, we can align ourselves with these processes and participate in the energetic flow of creation.

Annotated Bibliography (for this section)

Senge, Peter, *The Fifth Discipline: The Art and Practice of the Learning Organization*, Doubleday Currency, New York, NY., 1990

> This is the book that galvanized the field of organizational learning. In it Senge describes five essential disciplines: personal mastery, mental models, shared vision, team learning, and systems thinking which create an ethos of learning in an organization. These practices, which Senge demonstrates in a variety of contexts, enable an organization to discover the reality it is already operating by and then to recreate it for the sake of greater functionality and impact.

Kramer, Gregory, *Meditating Together, Speaking from Silence: The Practice of Insight Dialogue*, The Metta Foundation, Portland, OR, 1999

> This book reveals yet another application of the integral collective practice of dialogue. The author describes a particularly unique integration of the principles of dialogue with the mindfulness practices of Buddhism. He describes how insight dialogue can be employed to support *sangha* and to employ *sangha* to further the development of a form of mindfulness that extends into our social interactions.

Excerpted from Appendix B, "Study Guide,"
Embracing Life: Toward a Psychology of Interdependence,
David "Lucky" Goff, Ph.D., Mill City Press, 2013

Community as a Place for Discovery

— Lucky

If one stays on the growth track and continues to enlarge one's sense of self, the experience of community is inevitable. This is both good and bad news. The experience of wholeness, of knowing oneself to be part of the larger mystery of Life, is extremely gratifying. On the other hand, getting there and directly experiencing the flow of Life lets one in on the precariousness of Life. We teeter with it. Community brings this home to us and gives us access to the drama of the whole.

Community, the connection of all with all, is always present. In the background of our lives it is always there, always operating, affecting everything, dancing wildly. We are the direct descendants of this dancing mystery. Community calls us, like spawning salmon, back to our original waters, but we cannot get there on our own. In the effort to return to our home, to the place where we are actually begotten, we need each other.

The pursuit of community is the human equivalent of trying to live in harmony with Mystery. It is an effort that is itself mysterious. Like a good parent, this source calls us. Humans need to connect with each other to make this mystery palpable, to live in accord with it. As we near the source, we discover that we share a basic interdependence that connects us and that reaches into the complexity of creation.

Community, like evolution, is a conveyor belt. It delivers one, in a stage-by-stage way, to a deeper realization that the human bond is an echo of the larger dimension of connection that really animates all. This recognition is paradoxical and complex. We go through stages that include flesh and blood connections, intentional and unintentional.

Ripening in the sunlight of relationships and being buffeted around by those we come in contact with, we are prepared. Unfolding as we go, we become ourselves. In the process we discover there are many forms of community, many kinds of connections, some of which are shallow and some deeper. Each is a ground of preparation, a place of departure, and each is a home, a place where one can become. The dance of Life takes us through community, our ancestral home, the microcosm of the macrocosm we live in.

Defining Community

Humans have tried for millennia to define community. Most of these definitions have been one-dimensional. Community is a diverse phenomenon that suffers from a lot of different perceptions. In an effort to clarify what this chapter is about (the relational nature of our lives), community will be more thoroughly defined. A complex phenomenon that unfolds over time, community isn't just one thing. So defining it is a process of considering perspectives that change. As you will see, community has multiple guises.

Community is defined in many different ways. It is a complex social phenomenon that appears different depending upon how you are looking at it. For this reason it suffers from a lot of definitions. It is a confusing topic, but as you will see, one that has important implications for our species' wellbeing. Community can be seen as:

- An external and internal experience,
- A peak experience or an ongoing consciousness,
- A developmental or ripening perspective,
- A marketing tool.

External vs. Internal Experience

Community definitions have, until recently, dwelt primarily upon the surface, upon the outside of the experience. Community has been seen as a noun, a thing to be described. Attributes such as shared place (geography), values, and traditions have been evoked. Community thus seems like a worldly thing; but in fact it is also an unruly awareness, a process.

Community can also be a verb. Luckily, our understanding of community has evolved; it now reflects a nuanced and complex experience. Changes in the way we define community reflect how we have grown. Evolving has meant that other dimensions have become important, internal dimensions such as the quality of connection, the degree of meaningful interaction, mutual influence, and consciousness.

These definitions are attempts to capture and embody in everyday life the macrocosm of connection we live in. But community is much more than a wonderful set of interactions. It is a way of experiencing life. It is a mysterious state of consciousness in addition to a social structure. Community is confounding. Humans, despite our best attempts, cannot summon connection. We can only open to it. The process is always uncertain. And so we have a lot of confusion about this term.

Peak Experience or State of Consciousness

Some of the confusion around community is tied to the fact it can be both a peak experience and a state of consciousness. Community can be a discrete periodic experience generated by special conditions (such as emotionally compelling workshops), and it can be a stable, integrated awareness in the form of ongoing consciousness (a way of being connected).

The role community serves in providing an antidote to the fragmenting effects of modern life changes. Community as a discrete peak experience, can be like a booster shot supporting the immune system; or it can be, in its form as a state of consciousness, a permanent immunological resilience.

The form of connection one experiences determines the kind of world one lives in. Community is a complex phenomenon, which is hard to talk about because it changes as we change, as our perspective ripens and grows. Further confusion revolves around the way the degree of our ripeness favors and only perceives a particular form of community.

Development (or Ripening)

Research on human development indicates that humans tend to gravitate toward communities that operate in ways consistent with their development. This means that different types of groups, with different structures and capacities, appeal to folks with differing forms of consciousness. Community, then, is as diverse as we are.

What can be perceived as community is influenced by one's degree of ripeness (growth). We see only what we are prepared to see. Community, like the self, unfolds and changes as we become ourselves. Because it has many forms, this means that a particular form of community may not be right for everyone all the time. In fact, one way of distinguishing an honest community from a cult is how easily the members can come and go. A good community facilitates growth. It makes actualization for the collective's sake possible.

A Marketing Tool
Community is a confusing phenomenon because, in part, it is one of the true things treated like a mass-produced commodity. In the world of commerce a paradoxical element essential to human growth has been turned into a throw-away term, a kind of marketing come-on. The word "community" is used to describe all the users of a product (Microsoft User's community), those who share a common experience (the community of abused children), or those who share a common belief (the scientific community). Community has become a washed-out term. This degradation in the use of the word community reveals how far we have wandered away from caring about each other as fellow evolvers.

Community Endures
There is evidence that we have forsaken community and each other in service of the economy. But Life hasn't forsaken us. The inchoate desire for a group of like-minded companions is an echo of community and a vestigial awareness of how much we need each other to embody connection. The loss of community as a social ground has deep ramifications for us as a species. But an even greater reality is that Life has not given up on us. There is a continuum — of which we are a part — that hasn't changed.

Community still embodies connection; the Universe still operates as it has; we can still align ourselves. The loss of our natural social habitat hurts, but it simply asks us to be more conscious of how much we need each other. We need to be the social animals we are designed to be.

The Community of Affinity vs. the Community of Otherness

As we humans evolve, the world changes. Or so it seems. Actually, what is happening is that as we are growing our consciousness changes — and so does our way of making sense of what we perceive. It looks like the world is changing, but instead we are ripening. This is such a seamless development that it makes sense that we didn't really get it until recently. As we grow, we gain the ability to grasp more and more of the way things are. Community, the ground of our connectiveness, isn't entirely visible in all of its complexity at first. It becomes more palpable and correspondingly more complex as we grow the means to grasp what we perceive.

Community only truly, as a whole phenomenon, comes into sight in the later stages of human development. In the meantime, community is whatever we can handle at our present level of growth. If you remember, the early stages of human development are defined by the fact that we are animals, mammals, a herd species. As a result of our animal heritage we tend to look beyond ourselves for safety. This tendency shapes our early perception of community.

In the earliest stages of human growth we tend to be externally oriented; we look beyond ourselves for our wellbeing. Early on we favor the kind of community that emphasizes sameness, safety, and uniformity. Sociologists call this a community of affinity. Looking outside of ourselves we depend upon outside validation. Seeking similarity everywhere and having the experience of fitting in, is very gratifying emotionally, at least at first. Because we humans are on a developmental track, pushed onward by evolution, we have no idea early on that what feels so good now is going to be constricting soon.

The early stages of growth also temporarily satisfy the holonic tensions that bedevil us. By fitting in and preserving our nascent sense of self, it seems that we have found a home. And this is true for a while. But in that home the restlessness of the Universe is stirring. Soon similarity is going to feel stultifying and deadly. Community that emphasizes uniformity and the safe comfort of similarity slowly becomes a trap. What is happening is that the medium that once supported life and growth has succeeded, but it has grown a self that now needs another kind of environment to further honor the growth impulse within.

Early on humans need to be surrounded by the similar. This is a kind of developmental vulnerability. The marketplace capitalizes on this vulnerability by promoting products that seem to ensure that one will be acceptable, comfortable, and fit. Marketeers know that the earlier they can influence us with a look, style, product, or capability that seems to ensure a place in the herd, the more likely they can create a customer for life. Market forces create a false dependence. They do it by supplying an image, a surfacey, thin sense of self, which reduces (holonic) tension and temporarily replaces the more genuine and problematic evolving self.

This move is strategically good for the economy, but runs headlong into the process of evolution. Life is not invested in the market, but it is invested in us. The Universe needs us to become unique for it to expand. So the similarity of early life and the illusions of compatibility that the marketplace seems to offer, give way. Some are captured by this illusion. The market is effective, but only about a third of us have the temerity (or necessity) to look outside the huckster's tent. When this begins to happen, it isn't similarity but difference that becomes interesting.

Life likes diversity as much as it likes unity. Uniqueness boils away inside each of us. When the temperature is hot enough, a person starts to feel a desire to be around others who are different. The community of affinity gives way to the community of otherness. Like Goldilocks, the search is on for a life that contains "the just right" amount of otherness.

Early on, this isn't much difference; but later, as growth becomes a way of life, the more differences around the better. There is a spectrum of tolerance for differences that grows as we grow. Evolution seems to start at the conformity end, where difference is perceived as threatening, and grows to the other end, where difference is perceived as liberating and educative. There are lots of stages in between; more nuance than I want to get into here. Suffice it to say that becoming more human means giving up the safety of the herd, and the kind of community it provides for more personal responsibility, and the kind of community where unique self-expression occurs.

The ability to appreciate the *other* grows as one's uniqueness and personal responsibility grows. As a result, one's sense of community changes, incorporating more challenging differences. Both forms of community need to and do exist. Looking at two entirely different and yet essential forms of community, one can see why there is confusion about what community is. If one is inclined to look even harder, it is possible to see the way the developmental needs of our complex species are always met by a form of community. We as a species are held by our own kind, and in the process we are held by Life.

Ideological Communities

There are communities that try to embody difference and sameness. They are uniform within, but appear diverse. They are containers for worldviews, for particular ways of seeing things. Here I am referring to communities, social organisms, which endeavor to preserve and forward an ideology. This form of community is like a nature preserve where thought-forms, ideas, or a single world-view is preserved. In the ecology of ideas this can be important, as the more diversity of ideas the better; but in the spectrum of human development this can be a dangerous phenomenon.

Ideological communities serve the whole better than they serve the individual. They are good at preserving the integrity of an idea or worldview, but not so good at being places encouraging and supporting growth in members. There is a viewpoint within the community that defines its identity, and members are expected to adhere to it. It feels good finding such a group, because the need to fit is satisfied and one's worldview is validated. But change a little, and there is friction. In these types of communities there is a strong orthodoxy and usually lots of internal conflict that revolves around ideological purity.

Aloneness and Community

The quest for a true community of otherness often goes through an ideological group. Sometimes this can be a traumatic experience. People frequently feel hurt and disappointed by their experiences. This is an important part of the experience of community. As one moves developmentally toward fitting into a community that contains a greater degree of otherness, one needs to feel more comfortable alone. Growth in, and through, community contains paradox; to fit in one must be comfortable in one's own skin.

Community enfolds and supports development. Sometimes this happens through aloneness — the outsider experience; and sometimes it happens through feeling the fit pinch — the insider experience. In both cases loneliness occurs. One is at the same choice-point that occurs in all relationships. This is where human holons are forced to grow. Become yourself and face the possibility of rejection by others (and more aloneness), or reject the uniqueness growing within you in favor of fitting in (and feel the burn of being inauthentic).

Some people stop here. They try to regulate their growth to avoid this dilemma. Sometimes Life stands for this, sometimes not. Sometimes humans are thrust into and out of communities to satisfy something they have no control of. When this happens, otherness tolerance, because of what's happening within, grows.

Paradoxical forces are at work. Most of us can't bear them. There are fewer people around who are willing to explore the rigors and freedoms that growing introduces. As a consequence the community of otherness is more rare than the community of affinity. This is a difficulty. There are very few places where one can be idiosyncratically unique and still feel connected. This kind of diversity, a connected diversity, is essential to the development of our kind. It is, unfortunately, rare.

Intentional Community and Unintentional Community

Life goes on, however. The community of otherness that could help make sense of what is going on within, instead of serving as a practice field where one can learn more about being fully human, reverts to the unintentional community one is always a part of. The learning curve steepens; and in the midst of the chaos of fellow humans, we have the task of becoming ourselves.

Typically, there is a preference for what is called intentional community. This is the community phenomenon that comes closest to being a hybrid of affinity and otherness. Usually in these types of communities a certain desire for community is assumed. This results in common values such as consensus decision-making, non-violent communication, and shared conflict reduction processes. These types of communities represent something like the equivalent of self-selected marriages. The emphasis is upon growth within shared vows.

Intentional community has long been a social experiment, one that has embodied the desire to return to a previous era in our species' life. Intentional communities range from bearing a cultish orthodoxy to being places that breed connective awareness. They are like marriages; some work well, increasing love, and some lead into deadening ruts. They provide us with social experiments. They serve species' learning. They would seem to provide an option for the future; but in the meantime, another reality is unfolding.

Like it or not, most of us live the single life, disconnected from any one community and subject to the unintentional community that exists around us. This is also a great learning opportunity, but it poses as a field of uncaring, disconnected relationships. This is the community that life has selected for us. It is like an arranged marriage in that it still offers us the opportunity to find out how much connection we can bear. Unlike the re-assurance of similarity that seems to be available in the intentional community, the unintentional community offers a vivid experience of differing.

Unintentional community asks us to become ourselves in a cauldron that offers no reassurance, no illusion of sameness, no pretense of connection, no trust in pre-arranged processes of agreement, no assurance of being liked: just a vivid sense of going it alone.

Unintentional community is what passes for normalcy in most of our lives. It seems like an anathema to our wellbeing. And it is, to most of us. The majority of us who remain in the throes of looking for outside validation are going to find exposure to this teeming diversity very unpleasant. The experience seems much like being an unheld baby — it is hard to thrive. But for those rarer folk who have developed more responsibility for their own wellbeing, this mass of otherness is less daunting and more enlivening. The loss of certain kinds of community gives way to the gain of a broader, more complex, and more loosely defined form of community.

Unintentional community is still community. The matrix of relationships that stimulate our lives has not disappeared. Instead these relationships have just come into sight as something different. Most people see them and feel loss; they are gobbled up by the impersonal, non-validating nature of unintentional community. A few experience it as a more challenging home. Very few know that unintentional community is all there is, that the Universe buzzes with relationships that are not intended, obvious, or chosen. In another paradoxical shift that has dazzling implications, the loss of community (that seems coherent) introduces one to the deepest community of all, the life of the Universe.

Unintentional community is not a developmental preference. Before one gets there, ripens sufficiently, this omnipresent reality looks like the loss of community, the loss of connection. Instead, it is the ultimate community. Connection isn't dependent upon our development, but our ability to experience it is. Sometimes growing into ourselves introduces us to levels of reality we don't like. It is probable that this is the reason some people stop growing. It is too hard to bear a more complex and wild reality. Unintentional community is unwelcome in early developmental stages; but as we grow, it becomes a world where connection can come from any direction, and frequently does. Ripening brings us into contact with greater Mystery.

Remembering the Process of Becoming Community Creatures

To clarify, humans develop as they age. There is a spectrum of stages of growth in awareness that can occur. So, too, there is a spectrum of community forms that we prefer and are capable of. Because we are a mammalian species, we start out focused outside of ourselves. Safety, early on, means fitting into the herd and not being too distinct. The preferred form of community for these early, other-oriented times is some form of affinity community.

As individuals ripen, they grow more interested in becoming themselves. From the inside there grows an impulse toward uniqueness. This results in a growing preference for a social setting that embodies more differences. For these few souls, driven by this burst of uniqueness, there grows a preference for some form of community of otherness. Otherness grows more and more welcome as one becomes more and more unique.

Very few go even further. There is little support for this kind of development, but the fact that a few make it shows that the potential is within us. From having an external orientation, these few have made a developmental journey that goes all the way through being motivated exclusively for their own sakes to having a desire to relate as part of the larger whole. For these few to experience community in the midst of what most of us consider social chaos, they become more fully unique.

Unintentional connections occur for them because they are equipped to perceive lines of relationship. They have cultivated, through a combination of solitude (self-growth alone) and connection (self-growth in relationship) an awareness that is inside them, an awareness that enables them to relate to all beings. They are able to relate to all because they relate to the Mystery within. Essentially they have embodied that Mystery and therefore have gained the capacity internally to relate to the whole. Community (relationship) has become a way of being. It is an awareness that grasps the way things are.

The State of Community

I want to emphasize a painful reality that affects our everyday development. The loss of community is real. This is an important outcome of the lifestyle choices we as a species are making. In the west the feeling of being connected is rare now. The so-called developing world is slowly eliminating all forms of collective identity. The very survival of the things that have made us most human are in jeopardy. Community is our natural social environment. Any loss of community impacts upon the survival of our sense of connection. Human community has traditionally served as the intermediary that cultivated awareness of the individual's relationship with the Cosmos. Without being set in the tissue of connection, individuality becomes a corrosive thing for individual, nature, and society alike. (Connection with anything larger than the herd, then, is rarer and rarer.) This becomes a dangerous situation, much like we have today.

There are evolutionary costs associated with the loss of community. The losses are extensive. Basically, when humans live without the checks and balances of community, they end up with a doubly distorted reality. They don't perceive themselves or the world very accurately. This hurts. Nature has been paying the most overt price, but the cost is rebounding into the human world. The life that most individuals have today is subject to the worst suffering because of the loss of meaningful connection to the larger processes of Life. The worst of it is that we know this is an unsustainable course and that continuing it undermines confidence in all things human.

Happily, Life happens anyway. From its point of view nothing has really changed. We are still as connected as we have always been. We are still being put through the changes that come with connection. The thing is, humans are largely unable to see how these changes can be beneficial. They no longer know themselves to be holonic extensions of the life of the Universe.

There are those who lament the loss of community by pointing out that community loss has accompanied several hundred years of capitalism and the industrial revolution. It is true that this loss has taken place and in this context community skills seem to have eroded. But luckily,

Life has kept them alive. Humans may have failed to pay attention, but the context we find ourselves in has not changed. We have several thousands, perhaps millions, of years' experience with knowing Life, and with Life's help we can find a better way.

The opportunity to live in a more connected way is still present. Life has not abandoned us. The fact that we have put ourselves in a very hard situation only reflects how much we have forgotten what we really are. Life will go on; so can we, all we need do is remember we are connected and know we are desired. One of the best ways of doing that is to practice community. Community is the natural state of relationship that exists. Community is the growth-supporting social environment that brings out, and values, the unique contribution each of us makes to the expansion of the Universe.

Community and Self-development
Community — the sense of connection that is populated by people you know and who know you — has grown iffy. The result of living in a social environment where community barely exists is that self-growth also becomes iffy. Life keeps providing the stimulative dilemmas, but people without connection mainly feel these dilemmas are an imposition, a sign that something is wrong. Living without a connective intermediary such as community leaves humans vulnerable to the come-ons of the marketplace. Psuedo connections and virtual experiences replace the real thing. One is thrust further into a world constructed to make profits. The absence of genuine connection without any profit motive leaves one alienated and isolated.

Mystery, however, keeps unfolding, prodding us toward ripeness, toward becoming unique. This creates a difficulty. Currently there is a collision between what unfolds us and the absence of supports we have for this kind of ripening. Reality will win out; it usually does. In the meantime people will suffer, human potential will be lost, and the illusion of separation will continue. But the surge of Life will prevail.

We live with a false fear. Mistakenly, a lot of emphasis has been placed upon humanity's impact upon the environment. This obscures what is really happening, the source of our truest anxiety. We are killing ourselves. Through our impact on the environment we are creating a world that is inhospitable to us. Having forgotten our connection with the life of the Universe, we have lost our reason for living. We have forgotten how our existence is a miracle of Life.

This forgetting rebounds into our individual lives. It promotes conditions that neglect the Life surging through each one of us. The loss of connection with others in some form of community is a severing of connection with the larger reality. The challenges that come with becoming unique are truly daunting. The effort makes no sense if one is disconnected. These challenges seem like a major inconvenience. They are more; they are an indication of how desired one is. But the absence of community or the will to connect with other human beings beyond the family make this miraculous symmetry very hard to discover.

Going through the challenges involved with becoming unique involves a choice. It is a lonely choice. Life has set up this choice point. There is a lot more at stake than a merely human life. The expansion of the Universe, the viability of evolution, the integrity of the whole is present. Human existence is a form of Life's experimentation. Can human life be a step in the evolution of Life itself? Life goes on, it doesn't wait for us; but our holonic nature ensures that we can be a part of what goes on.

Relationship and Community

Living in a field of relationships is living in a type of community. The more one is capable of opening to relatedness, the more one is able to participate in, and perceive, this community. Every step one takes in one's development not only matures one, but increases the likelihood that connection becomes more palpable. Slowly opening, embracing oneself, automatically means embracing more and more of the connections that sustain. Life is like that. The current assumption is separation and aloneness, but that is only how things look from our current scientific perspective. Life presides in its own way.

Ripening entails opening to what is, while becoming true. This is a collaborative process. Life is a partner, a partner with a big investment.

It never leaves us alone. Relationship is its leverage, its way of making sure this investment is a good one. The checks and balances of community shape us, with or without our awareness.

Community, the kind we humans make, is considered difficult. Community, the kind Life makes, is ubiquitous. This disparity is hard to bear. It reveals our unused potential, the growth in front of us, a possible future we could choose. Life has set up the possibility, the inevitability for some species. Are we going to be that species? No one knows for sure. Awareness of this is hard. Home is still beyond our reach, even though it crowds in on us in the form of others.

Community seems like an option, a lifestyle choice. One marries because one wants to or because family expects it. So, people believe they can enter, or not enter, the complex field of relatedness that is community. Not so. Community is an inevitability. One can practice now, consciously, and learn through bearing the difficulty of connecting with others; or one can live the consequences of being connected and pretending otherwise. Each offers suffering and rewards. Which, however, offers the best chance to grow and serve the whole?

There is a consequence of connection. Community makes it too explicit, not just as a demand, but as a relational responsibility. There really is no free lunch. Being connected means that things are going to be asked of us. We can play along or not, but we cannot avoid our communal chores. That is the good and bad news. The consequences are not ours to make entirely, and they will come. We are wanted and needed. Life asks much of us. Our lives are our response. Community lies in the connection of the two.

Communitas

There is a kind of communal wisdom that is very rare today. This wisdom is the product of residing together, in one place, for a long time. It is an old wisdom. I don't know if we have an equivalent for our modern, fast paced, technologically connected, global village. One anthropologist, when he encountered it, called it *communitas*. He was referring to a kind of collective awareness of unity that was generated through a community ritual. It seems that some indigenous people had developed the communal self-awareness that led to periodic events, collective rituals, that reminded them how connected they were.

To infuse their society with meaning and connection they put together periodic rites intended to help them maintain their sense of being meaningfully connected to the Cosmos and each other. In other words they deliberately reminded themselves that their relationship with each other, their sense of community, was related to their sense of place in Creation.

Earlier societies seem to have developed the awareness that the bond that gave a culture a sense of connection had to be tended and periodically renewed. We could use that kind of awareness today. Just as we know that marital vows thrive when they are periodically renewed, we need to create events that make explicit the relational conditions that shape our lives. These events don't have to happen all the time, just frequently enough that they serve to remind us that we are here together and all share the same basic fate.

In indigenous cultures these kinds of events attracted everyone. Our ancestors lived in a world that wasn't so socially stratified; the people had a sense of equality that was a product of living together in relationship to Mystery. We don't know each other, keep moving, stay busy, live in different social circles, and limit our contact with each other. But Life accompanies us anyway. The hardships that made the old collective rituals come to life are still here. Cancer, accidental death, or some other form of mishap, can befall anyone. In the eyes of Life we are all equal. Community exists, and we can become aware of it.

This awareness comes through our individual ripening, but there is a social way of knowing and supporting such growth. Connection still prevails. Periodically recalling this aspect of who we are, our common humanity in the face of a mysterious Universe helps us all to know and assume our place in Creation. Community, our relationship home, is never far away, no farther than our awareness can take us. True, it does take will to go there, but that will is not just our own.

Humankindness

The word that describes this section, humankindness, says it all. All of the growth and ripening leads, as some of our ancestors knew, to recognizing all of our relationships as important. Relations with our fellow humans carried a special significance because they were a reflection of our relationship with the Mystery within us. We treat them as we do, because that is how we treat ourselves. Reverence for the Mystery unfolding within, as us, means reverence for the Mystery unfolding within others.

Humankindness is a word coined by the same cultural anthropologist that gave us the word *communitas* to describe the sense of oneness that could bind a community. With humankindness he was attempting to describe the attitude some indigenous people had toward others. This word describes an attitude that is not merely a moral stance, it is an attitude taken because of a vivid experience. They knew they were in a world of deep connections, which included, as part of the same spectrum, strangers as a part of their relations.

This is a realization based upon development. It is an experience that comes with a rare ripeness, one we are capable of, but rarely get to because we lack the supports and the vision of what is possible for us. Community has traditionally been the medium that delivered us to this awareness. For only by being around others in a deep and complex way can one grow the essential internal relationship skills that are necessary to see the kinship between yourself and another.

Humankindness is bivalent; it has two aspects that are important. There is a sense of kinship. This is an existential realization. The other is my sibling, a fellow journeyer, another being subject to the same vulnerable uncertainty of existence. I and the other are alike. We are the same kind. Because this is so, and because I have the ability to open myself to the Mystery within, I can do so with the mystery of another. This is an opening I am capable of choosing because I do so in my everyday life. I know how to be kind in response to the Mystery of everyday life.

Many indigenous people lived in enclaves of similarity. They never had to learn to embrace the surprising benefits and hardships available in the community of otherness. Some had other experiences. They have shown us what is possible. Today humankindness awaits the few who can weather the rigors of aloneness in the crowd and who develop the capacity to see what our human experiences hold in common. Relationship reality awaits our realization and binds us as we find our way back to our relationship home. Humankindness evolves as we approach that home.

Community and True Things

Humans live in a frothing soup of connective relationships. This isn't evident at first. As we ripen more and more into the uniquenesses we are, we become increasingly capable of opening ourselves more to the relationships that stimulate and shape us. Community seems more omnipresent as we change. Our preferences, perceptions, and capacity to embrace diversity grow with us. As they do, the backdrop becomes more palpable.

Along the way many forms of community appear and recede. All along we are connected. All along, this connection is troublesome. It generates a lot of ambivalence in us. Learning how to cope with connective challenge isn't easy. Living in a cultural time where connection is denied makes it hard to see what really challenges. But Life isn't really stopped by this. It keeps serving up the challenges needed to maximize and ensure uniqueness. It lives in community with us while we learn to live in community with it.

The experience of being embedded in something larger is one of the true things. Community makes this reality more palpable to us. The struggle to connect with others is another version of the struggle we have with connecting with our evolving selves. Each is wild, changing, challenging, and mysterious. The fact is, and this accounts for our natural ambivalence, the unknown resides at the center of both.

Community is the true thing that most thoroughly asks us to go beyond ourselves and provides the conditions for us to discover another, more complex version of ourselves in the process. It is the very rich, relational complexity of community that slowly generates an increasing complexity in our awareness. Human consciousness became complex enough to generate self-reflection because we are social animals embedded in a complex set of relationships. We became the aware animals we are because of community. Our consciousness was born in community. Our continued growth depends upon this same context.

Community on the human level mirrors the larger reality of connection that surrounds us. The slow erosion of community feeling, the decline of communal identity, the loss of community experiments, all reveal a cultural world that has lost touch with its context. The marketplace contributes to this skewed vision. So does an over-reliance on the findings of science. Relationship, community feeling, is not a visible, tangible thing that can be measured and given a value. The loss of community feeling, of human enclaves that practice it, of valuing the intangibility of connection reveals the way we are choosing to go on without Life. Luckily, Life isn't giving up on us.

Community is not a commercial enterprise. No amount of money will create these valuable connections. In essence we are community animals. The way to a deeper sense of this is through opening up the self. There are rigors involved in that kind of opening. To experience what is always there, to be capable of connecting deeply with others, one must be prepared to learn, to be vulnerable, uncertain, and to go beyond the known self. That is a tall order, one that cannot be bought. Community connects us all, but we have to grow ourselves to know it. Many virtues come into play when we finally do. The most important of these is becoming a part of a greater whole, gaining our true connective inheritance.

Last section from Chapter 8 of *True Things: Redeeming What Money Cannot Buy,*
—David "Lucky" Goff, Ph.D. not published as of April, 2014

ॐ

WISDOM

Wisdom does not inspect, but beholds.

— *Thoreau*

Wisdom Quotes & Commentaries

There is a wisdom of the head, and ... a wisdom of the heart.
— *Charles Dickens*

There are many forms of wisdom. As I have been thinking about wisdom I have found myself swimming in deeper and deeper waters. I didn't come to this inquiry into the nature of wisdom because I am wise (this is probably a fool's errand), but because I wanted to become wiser. I am discovering that becoming wiser is a journey to the frontier, to the place where what is not-known becomes known. I am also discovering that I don't possess any knowledge until I actually live something out. In my mind, there is no wisdom unless it comes from experience.

To give an example of different forms of wisdom, Dickens mentions wisdom of the heart differs from wisdom of the head. I believe him, but only because I have experienced the truth of his assertion. Later I will address what I think he means, but for the moment I want to discuss another important difference which impacts whether I perceive wisdom or not.

I believe there is a difference between the wisdom of the ages and the wisdom of the moment. I tend to think developmentally. For me, that means that I see human beings unfolding in a somewhat predictable manner over time. I think we evolve like other complex organisms in a stage-by-stage manner. The wisdom of the moment is the wisdom determined by the stage of development one is in. To function fully in any stage you need to have a sense of what is the best wisdom of that stage. That means someone has put into words the quintessential nature of that stage. The wisdom of the moment captures the best qualities and outlook of where you are.

This means that one person's wisdom might be another person's idiocy. A fool may not be wrong because wisdom is really different at different stages. This form of wisdom also differs from what I call wisdom of the ages. This kind of wisdom is trans-developmental, to me that means it is true at all of the levels, or wise no matter how developed one is. This form of wisdom has lasting value. That is why I call it wisdom for the ages. All too often, what passes for the wisdom of the ages is the wisdom of a particular stage, preferably the stage one is currently occupying. This leads to confusion about what wisdom really is. And it leads to heartache, confusion, and misdirected effort.

As much as possible, I want to explore the kind of wisdom that endures and is true no matter where one is. But I, too, am human, which means that I occupy some developmental level that will make what I think wise, suspect. The wisdom I extol will say much about me and may not really address what you think wise. I can't escape from this limitation on my view, but I can be mindful of it, and warn you about it. True wisdom is, in my mind, the wisdom that lasts. This is the wisdom I'm really after. But it is a form of wisdom I may or may not recognize. Wisdom, mine or yours, may or may not appear in a form that is desirable to us both. So be forewarned, and let's proceed.

Dicken's recognition that the heart and the head have different forms of wisdom is true, some of the time. So, despite the truth of what he says, I would consider this form of wisdom to be the wisdom of the moment. There are other forms of wisdom that contradict this one. For instance Frank Lloyd Wright has said, "The heart is the chief feature of a functioning mind." His configuration of wisdom suggests that the two forms of wisdom are best integrated. Both forms reflect different perspectives that are true, at least some of the time. They represent to me a kind of wisdom that is provisional, partial, and only momentarily true.

I want there to be some other kind of wisdom, a kind I can count on, that is always true. But, I am aware of Nils Bohr's saying that "The opposite of a fact is a lie. And the opposite of a great truth is another great truth." This form of wisdom sets me spinning. It seems wisdom may be somehow paradoxical. If this is true, then there is the possibility that if I get what I want out of this inquiry, I may not be getting what I want. And, that if I don't accomplish what I want by doing this inquiry, I may be accomplishing what I want. This is a kind of wisdom I don't think I am equipped to handle, and it may be the kind of wisdom that is best able to inform me.

Paradoxical thinking changes the form of wisdom. I need to notice this. Wisdom is evasive; it changes form as we grow. Maybe there is no form of wisdom that can be reliably counted on to express the wisdom of the ages, except that wisdom changes. What is wisdom if it changes?

I don't like where this is leading. Wisdom is more complex than I am. The elusiveness of what I seek seems to lead me deeper into the woods and ensures that I get lost there. Searching for wisdom, seeking to be wiser, is delivering me into a world that I really don't know. Am I wiser for being lost? I don't really know, but what I am experiencing is that I can only know wisdom if I give up thinking I know anything. I'm not sure that is a deal I'm willing to make, or even can make.

I heard a quote from Einstein. He is seen as a genius, one of the rare ones who seemed to possess some sort of sight or wisdom. I can't repeat his words verbatim, but they amount to this: a man of great spirit (and presumably great wisdom) is quite often violently opposed by men of mediocre minds. In his mind it seemed that wisdom could be dangerous. One could know something that is intolerable to someone else. What is worse is that it seems like the wiser one gets, the more likely one is to know something that is intolerable to others. The search for knowledge, if this is true, is dangerous and for either the very courageous or the very foolish. I think I am more the latter than the former.

I am going to proceed very cautiously. I realize I am going into a morass that will very likely kill or change me. I would like to emerge. I would like to have something to say. But if I truly get wiser, if I encounter real wisdom and it wises me up, then it is likely that if and when I return, I will wisely have nothing to say.

Wisdom seems to be deadly, dangerous, and more rare than I formerly believed. I'm not sure how much I really want it. I am somewhat sure that I may not be able to handle it. It seems likely, and you should be forewarned about this, that I am only likely to retain and recognize wisdom I can handle. This is probably true for you, too, dear reader. I count myself as having done what I set out to do, shared my investigation of wisdom with you, if you, as well as I, are disturbed by what is revealed.

If we are to hold solitude and community together as a true paradox, we need to deepen our understanding of both poles. Solitude does not necessarily mean living apart from others; rather, it means never living apart from one's self. It is not about the absence of other people — it is about being fully present to ourselves, whether or not we are with others. Community does not necessarily mean living face-to-face with others; rather, it means never losing the awareness that we are connected to each other. It is not about the presence of other people — it is about being fully open to the reality of relationship, whether or not we are alone.

—*Parker Palmer* from *A Hidden Wholeness:*
The Journey Toward An Undivided Life —Welcoming the Soul
and Weaving Community in a Wounded World

The opposite of a fact is a lie. The opposite of a great truth is another great truth.

— *Neils Bohr*

Take your well-disciplined strengths
and stretch them between two opposing poles,
because inside human beings,
is where
God learns.

— *Rilke*

Wisdom is, or can be, a paradox. It can be contradictory and elusive. I like the idea of learning what these wisdom quotes evoke. I tend to think the wisdom that is truly wise will wise me up. But then these quotes also evoke the idea of holding onto yourself. I'm not sure I can do that and never lose the awareness that is evoked in me. Wisdom, it seems (or at least some forms of wisdom), asks something of me. It seems to be asking me to hold on (to myself) while at the same time it is asking me to let go, and be carried to a new way of looking at things. Holding on and letting go: these seem to be contradictory capacities. Can I do both?

It seems that the process of acquiring wisdom, and not just being exposed to it, is demanding. Apparently, some forms of wisdom lie "between two opposing poles," where if I "stretch" myself I can access them. Growing wiser, learning something, seems to require that I acquire something, perhaps a kind of anticipatory fertility, like the fecundity of a plowed field, ready for seeding.

Strangely, this "something" seems to reside in the space I can only inhabit if I am willing to stretch myself and become more complex than I usually am. The challenge seems to be that I must make myself ready (to be seeded), open to possibility without giving myself up, without leaning too far towards what I want.

Wisdom hunting is arduous. I have to grow myself to acquire wisdom. That seems fair and unfair. I don't think I would value the acquisition of wisdom if I didn't have to work for it. On the other hand, I'm tired of always having to become more just to get something. Wisdom, it seems to me, should be available no matter what. Wisdom seems too wise to just be available to me as I am, instead it seems to ask me to change. I don't like this very much, but I do respect it for doing so.

This seems especially true about the paradoxical forms of wisdom. I think it is always true that I have to grow myself in order to acquire wisdom, but it seems that paradoxical wisdom requires me to more consciously and deliberately grow myself. I have to value myself and subject myself to the rigors of growing if I am going to really acquire anything. This actually requires a kind of self-regard that is genuinely more self-sacrificing than I have ever been. To get to be wise enough to handle paradox, I have to do the paradoxical. I have to hold onto and let go of myself at the same time.

Wow! Wisdom protects the integrity of itself by requiring growth. This seems like a just and infuriating reality. Real wisdom is only implied by wisdom quotes. To get wise one has to go through something. Wisdom is experiential. I want more wisdom in my life, but I'm not sure I want to pay full price for it; although I know if I do, that I will be more than ever before. The price is high, but so is the quality I achieve. This is a deal I cannot make unwittingly. The price is too great and the value too important.

Paradoxical wisdom cannot be gained by the unwise. To get to the place where this kind of wisdom resides one must become wise enough. This growth is like one of those video games that requires new skills to achieve new levels. Practice and failure are part of the way. No wonder this kind of wisdom is so rare. Who wants to fail enough to get there?

Paradoxical wisdom is nice to know about, but not so nice to acquire. It exists, beguilingly, but it asks so much that it seems super human. It isn't, but it might as well be. Seeing both sides is possible, even desirable; but being capable of it means developing all sides of oneself, and that is not an easy thing to do. Wisdom protects itself, I mean its integrity, by calling out and making demands. I can only foolishly go so far. Wisdom prevents me from going further unless I am truly willing to pay the price — not in terms of currency, but in terms of self.

Wisdom is exactly proportional to the size of the group one is responsible for.

— *Mihalyi Czesentmihalyi*

Wisdom is a sacred communion.
— *Victor Hugo*

It is great folly to wish to be wise all alone.
— *Francois de La Rochefoucauld*

The next best thing to being wise oneself is to live in a circle of those who are.

— *C.S. Lewis*

There is often an overlooked social dimension to wisdom. It is widely understood that wisdom serves us, that it has a more collective, widespread impact. What is less understood is that wisdom emanates from collective sources. Access to this form of wisdom is social. It takes more than one.

Social wisdom comes because, as Dickens pointed out, the wisdom of the heart is involved. Caring gives one entrée into the world of connection. In that world wisdom of the heart thrives. This wisdom isn't just the product of a single heart though; it is the wisdom of hearts linked by caring. The wisdom seems to come through these linkages. In other words it doesn't seem to be a product of the hearts themselves, but of the linkages. This form of wisdom seems to be an emergent quality; it seems to be something that is co-created.

This is a special category of wisdom. We usually think about wisdom coming from a wise person, a woman or a man. But, in this case, we are talking about a kind of wisdom that comes from a wisely connected assemblage of some sort. Here it is the quality of the connection as well as those involved that allows the wisdom to be created. Meaningful, heartfelt connection generates something that moves people. We all know it's possible, but few of us really expect it and try to cultivate it.

What is the nature of social wisdom? What does it have to teach us about ourselves, about how best to occupy this world?

There are many questions that arise by virtue of awareness of a social dimension of wisdom. They emerge from Czesentmihalyi's assertion that connection and responsibility for others generates wisdom, to Hugo's sense that wisdom is a "sacred communion." It is better not to be wise alone and to have a wise group to turn to. There is something about being connected with others that is wisdom-producing and wise.

One thing that seems to generate wisdom is perspective. A reason why wisdom is difficult to achieve is because it is easy to get trapped in one's perspective. The more perspective, the more likely wisdom becomes. Gaining access to the perspective of others seems to be a good way to broaden one's own perspective. I suspect that the assertion that responsibility is important brings home the awareness that perspective is more than "seeing" and "understanding." Real perspective comes from something deeper, from walking in someone else's shoes.

Social wisdom, which is the wisdom arising from our social nature, seems to have something to do with the perspective that is available when the circle enlarges. As one becomes many, perspective grows and wisdom becomes more likely. What is interesting about this form of wisdom is that it doesn't seem to arise as a result of numbers increasing, but of caring increasing. A large group, or any group, is not intrinsically wise, but if people care about each other and care about what they are doing together, then they are more likely to use their perspective to increase wisdom.

Social wisdom not only exists, but seems to arise from the quality of connection occurring within a group. Caring is apparently a high quality form of responsibility, that expands perspective and raises awareness. Social wisdom seems to follow. This form of wisdom seems to be wise because it expresses what we are capable of together. And if this wisdom be true, then apparently we are capable of quite a lot.

ॐ

Never mistake knowledge for wisdom. One helps you make a living; the other helps you make a life.

— Sandra Carey

To recognize the significant in the factual is wisdom.

— Dietrich Boenhofer

The saddest aspect of life right now is that science gathers knowledge faster than society gathers wisdom.

— Isaac Asimov

Knowledge comes, but wisdom lingers.

— Alfred Lord Tennyson

The art of being wise is the art of knowing what to overlook.

— William James

The greatest obstacle to discovery is not ignorance — it is the illusion of knowledge.

— Daniel J. Boorstin

Knowledge isn't wisdom. That is a simple statement. One that is believable, but one that seems so far from what is normal in our cultural world. I don't know about you, but I live in a world where we seem to celebrate the knowledgeable as if they are the wise ones. It seems as if the more one knows the more one is consulted with. If wisdom is not a function of knowledge, then what are we doing with so many graduate programs?

The advent of information technology seems to suggest that wisdom lies somewhere on the continuum of knowledge. The more info one has at his or her disposal, the better prepared one is for life. Right. Well, no. Not if wisdom really is something else. I've heard it said that Life doesn't care how much one knows, it only cares about who one is. This seems to capture some awareness that wisdom is composed by the nature of the inside of a human life rather than by outside showiness. Knowledge is in fact hollow without the depth of experience to recognize the real significance of something.

Wisdom comes out of intelligence, but it is intelligence tempered by the fire of experience. Knowledge can be merely abstract knowing, Knowledge may cover a wide area, but it also is a thin, surfacey, phenomenon. It can appear deep, but it collapses into a kind of pretense before a real dilemma. To go beyond the moment, to go forward in a situation that calls for real innovation and creativity, one needs the confidence that is generated by having faced the difficult and unknown before.

Wisdom is knowledge plus experience, and experience is the most important factor. There is no substitute for having been adequately challenged. Wisdom is experiential, it is truly known, not just mentally, but with every fiber of one's being. Wisdom is as much an internal phenomenon as an external one. That means that the truly wise person is bringing their being to a situation and not just their knowing. Wisdom is located within, as a part of the whole person, instead of just being a function of the head.

Having knowledge is good and important. The world needs the knowledgeable. But it needs even more the even rarer wise person. Knowledge can pass for, and even obscure wisdom. In that sense knowledge can pose a danger to wisdom. Knowledge can give the impression of wisdom. This is a common deceit in a world that believes that information is power. The knowledgeable may look like they know something, and in that sense obscure the real truth of the moment by acting as if what is known is great enough to deal with the mystery of the moment. Knowledge is always composed by the past; wisdom, on the other hand, is available to the future.

Knowledge is good. It is reliable, trustworthy, and predictable. Knowledge is the almanac, the friend who keeps one alive by predicting the storms that will return again. Wisdom is something else. It is the confidence to face an uncertain future. They are not the same. They are similar in that they both embody a kind of knowing, but they are different because one is a knowing of the world and the other is a knowing of the self in the world. Wisdom is rarer because the self is such a mystery and surprisingly the world is easier to know. Wisdom resides in not-knowing; knowledge resides in the illusion of knowing.

Knowing others is intelligence; knowing yourself is true wisdom.
Mastering others is strength; mastering yourself is true power.

The well bred contradict other people. The wise contradict themselves.
— *Oscar Wilde*

The only true wisdom is in knowing you know nothing.
— *Socrates*

The fool doth think he is wise, but the wise man knows himself to be a fool.
— *William Shakespeare*

A man only becomes wise when he begins to calculate the approximate depth of his ignorance.
— *Gian Carlo Minotti*

Life is the only real counselor; wisdom unfiltered through personal experience does not become a part of the moral tissue.
— *Edith Wharton*

Knowing others is wisdom; knowing yourself is enlightenment.
— *Lao Tzu*

There is a personal, idiosyncratic nature to wisdom. Wisdom resides in a specific person, not like something that is kept, but as an aspect of being. As we know, wisdom is not a thing, it isn't something that can be drawn on, cultivated, or that runs out. Wisdom seems to be as deep as its host. How can it be present and not be a thing? How can wisdom emerge into the world without being a pool of light that exists somewhere?

It seems that wisdom is some kind of awareness that comes through self-knowledge. The wise are often humble because they know of the limitations, contradictions and discrepancies that accompany their existence. Wisdom seems to emerge from this kind of awareness.

The self seems to be an important ingredient in the emergence of wisdom. But wisdom doesn't merely come with having a self; it seems to be formed through looking deeply into that self. Wisdom evolves with self-scrutiny. Paying attention to the something that stirs within seems to arouse awareness that is wise. There is this apparent, though unobvious, link between what exists within and wise sensibilities. This idea, that wisdom has to do with having a relationship with the self, the mystery growing within, cuts across conventional thinking. The self is usually seen as troublesome, unruly, and selfish. How can an absorption in having things be the way wanted turn into a fountain spewing wisdom? There must be some strange alchemy at work here. There is. People become wise because they don't take themselves for granted; they look into what they are. The process of looking and being altered by what one sees creates a special kind of awareness.

The mystery of existence lies within. By and large, most of us are not really interested in knowing ourselves and the mystery of our existence. Really getting self-acquainted is unsettling. This is the main reason we aren't a wiser culture. Wisdom isn't very widespread because there are a host of challenges associated with self-awareness. The greatest is connected with liking what you find. There is a wilderness within that harbors a wild being, someone who is both human, plagued by limitations and fears, and a wondrous miracle, a being who is a microcosm of the greater macrocosm.

Wisdom emanates from the contradictory and puzzlingly paradoxical nature of this being. Life has created an enigmatic being that graces the Universe while it fumbles around. This is not how we are programmed to see ourselves. So when this paradoxical creature shows up, especially so close to home, there is a tendency to shut down, to hide. Only a few, the truly intrepid, keep looking. Wisdom comes from bearing the tension of a vivid experience of the dual nature of our humanity.

Looking within, deeply within, one becomes wise. Gazing at the self is not navel gazing, if it is an earnest effort, it is exposing oneself to

Mystery. This is a life-transforming endeavor. It usually doesn't come easily. One works at it, and when it does come, the wildness turns into wisdom, and that wisdom takes one deeper into the world.

Self-scrutiny is a lonely pursuit. It has its rewards and its challenges. Wisdom may manifest as an everlasting truth; it may even fit for all of us, most of the time; but often it is highly bound to the moment, specific, and sometimes ruthless. Being able to bear what wisdom asks takes a lot of self. One has to know the symmetry between the wise one within and the one who occupies this fragile and precarious life. That kind of self-knowledge isn't won in the lottery, it is found in the dark crevices of a lonely heart.

Elders and Wisdom

—Lucky

There is an ancient assumption that old people have wisdom. Assumptions often are dangerous. The danger can lie in assuming that that is all there is. There are, however, two forms of wisdom. Only one is accessible to the run of the mill old person. Old people in general typically hold the known wisdom of the past. This form of wisdom is precious and must be preserved. Old people are worth honoring simply because they have this form of hard-earned wisdom.

The assumption that old people are wise contains a logic that is hard to refute. The older one is, the more likely one has gone through something, which imparts some hard-earned knowledge. The old then are privy, by virtue of their life-experience, to a kind of wisdom. I call it "known wisdom." Known wisdom is based on experience, is rooted in the past, and is predictable.

Being old, however, is not enough to insure that old people have access to another form of wisdom. I call this form "unknown wisdom." Unknown wisdom is new, rooted in the present or future, and is unpredictable. If you will, this is the wiser wisdom, derived from the unknown, and only available to those who are comfortable with "not knowing." Elders, as opposed to merely old people, are the ones most likely to have access to this form of wisdom.

From this perspective then, there is an important distinction to be made between the wisdom needed, and the old people it is gotten from. Both forms of wisdom, known and unknown, are necessary and contributive, but one, unknown wisdom, is less known, harder to achieve, and more rare. Our species' survival depends upon both. Old folks give us access to both, but only the true elder has the necessary maturity to access the latter. This essay is designed to make that distinction evident. It is hoped that in so doing, unknown wisdom will become more prevalent, and elders will become more visible.

Growing Older

Each of us does what comes naturally to us. Despite anti-age creams and research that seeks "eternal life," we age. No amount of social privilege, money, or education changes and prevents aging. Life has its way with everyone, transforming each being into the greying, frailer version of itself. Humans have a life cycle that is growing in length now, but remains terminal. Aging comes upon each of us, and when it does, each of us demonstrates what we have learned at the hands of our kind. Thus, we arrive as grey beings in the form that nature conceived us, and shaped to some extent by the relations we've had.

Relationships are important to the elderly for a variety of reasons, extending from the relational attitudes of loved ones through the cultural attitudes that pass for conventional knowledge. Each shapes reality a little and can put an elderly person into a world that honors and affirms their natural development or treats them like an inconvenient problem. Growing older involves a perilous journey into the hands of others. By and large, the culture I'm an inhabitant of has not looked favorably on the old. It transmits a bias toward the young that renders aging precarious. The old, despite the need for relationships that are supportive and sustaining, are left on their own, barely supported and largely unseen.

Growing old creates suffering in some cultures. As we shall see, those cultures, where old people are not supported, suffer too. The lack of cultural support translates into a loss of wisdom and knowledge. Aging may come naturally to our kind but our cultural attitudes don't. This leaves the old people to themselves and hobbles them with attitudes that they have inherited from their culture.

It is no wonder that aging is not looked forward to and that it is seen as a form of decline. It is a wonder that some old folks have preserved their vitality and reveal other possibilities. These grey haired ones show us an alternative, a cultural possibility, which can return wisdom and knowledge to us all. Growing older for some people is a struggle to preserve their freedom. These old folks have found ways of staying true to themselves, freeing themselves from cultural attitudes that diminish them, preserving their wisdom and knowledge.

Growing older is an adventure. Much is learned in the process. Knowledge of the self, the culture one lives in, the choices that Life requires, and about Life itself alter the old person's perspective. These are changes in the point of view that could be of widespread use. In some cultures the insights of the old are valued; in some they aren't. This has an effect upon old and young alike. Growing older is a natural, inevitable process that happens to all, but all of the wisdom and knowledge this phase of human life contains is not available to all. This creates painful distortions and cuts some people and cultures off from important aspects of human experience.

When considering growing older and the growth of human wisdom and knowledge, one must look deeply into the prevailing cultural attitudes of a society. Aging is natural, but cultural beliefs can distort what is natural and render wisdom rare. The way the old of a culture are treated tells a lot about how mature that culture is. Wisdom is more available in a culture that honors its own maturity. All of this wealth of experience is squandered by some societies, but the wisdom continues to exist. To take advantage of it means going beyond the bad advice of the culture. This going beyond cultural blindness means seeing essential distinctions. Here is what I mean.

Elders vs. Merely Olders

There is a difference between people who merely get old and people who become elders. Known wisdom is available to both. Wisdom of the unknown sort, however, is more available to the latter. There is a host of distinguishing factors that sets old people apart, but they are all disguised by one similarity: that our ageist culture prevents most people from identifying elders. Both are old, wrinkled, grey and losing some faculties. The old are treated democratically alike; they are uniformly de-valued. When they are looked to for wisdom, they are all treated the same, and the unknown wisdom that elders have access to is to frequently overlooked.

In the following pages I try to make evident the way that Life has conspired with human consciousness to make an elder different from a merely old person. Don't misunderstand. Both are needed. Each carries an important awareness. But elder awareness and the kind of wisdom available to it is important to us because it carries our prospects. The future of humanity is unfolding right now. As elders delve into the unknown, the orbit of our kind is expanding. Tomorrow's possibilities are coming into view, a view that exists because elders make it available. So, it is important to know they are around and to know what they are capable of. After all, they will be some of us soon.

Maturational Differences

The journey from child to elder is a wild ride. It has many turning points, many ways to get off on another track. This is the primary reason that out of a growing number of old people only some of them are elders. Simply surviving the twists and turns of Life, though worthy of respect, isn't the same as thriving with a growing complex awareness. This awareness takes shape through weathering many storms, through experiencing heartaches and choosing to live one's life for the sake of the whole. Aging is an organic journey, but not everybody learns to thrive. Life, for the true elder, is a miracle that has implications for all.

Elders arrive at old age differently from the average old person. They are more self-possessed, more interested in others, less emotionally reactive and judgmental, more compassionate, and eager to serve the larger communities they feel themselves to be part of. They are motivated more from the inside out rather than the outside in. They are more self-confrontive and treat themselves and Life better. They know what their purpose is. Elders are humble; they know they are older and wiser because of life experiences and hardships. They are who they are because Life made them that way. They are the ones who have learned the alchemical trick of turning lemons into joyous lives.

This kind of development is rare because too few know of it, and because we currently have no cultural supports for it. Elders pass amongst us, and like most old people, are ignored, unseen, and mis-valued. They have actualized some of our human potentials. They could reveal a lot about what we are capable of. But, caught up in a consensus trance, brought on by our penchant for valuing the young and staying economically active, we miss what they have to offer and the world of possibility they point to.

They made it through the maturational change points that bring out our human potential. We could learn from the difficulties they have faced. After all, they are the way-showers, the ones who have turned the travails of Life into something that can serve us all. They do it because they face the difficulties of living, and they find the ways to convert those difficulties into assets.

We are going to lose capabilities, to need others, to be sick and infirm, to die. Maybe we could learn what elders seem to know — that being human is a challenging blessing.

Choosing

Elders embrace challenge because they recognize its role in Life. This isn't some kind of Pollyanna choice on their part. It is an act of deliberately turning and facing the music. Choosing, as practiced by an elder, is putting one's life on the line. This kind of choosing is activism. What elders do involves real risk.

Invariably, this kind of choosing is anxiety-provoking. We live in a time where anxiety and apprehension are treated like they are options that tend to indicate something is wrong. People stop growing to avoid anxiety. The anxiety-phobic nature of our culture often translates into anxiety intolerance. Many choose anything else. This leads to shallow individuals and an immature culture. Facing the music means pressing on. Pressing on means marching into a lonelier world, where friends are rare, and understanding is even rarer.

Growing Through Pain and Loss

Elders are familiar with loss, hardship and pain. They have been grown by what they have been through. Here is another potential stopping place; growing pain. Many older people are besieged by pain. They stop growing because of it. Conventional thinking would imply pain is an option. The difficulties of Life can be avoided with the right painkiller or anti-depressant. For the elder, learning is steep and rapidly gets personally uncomfortable. The willingness to experience pain for the sake of growth is a hallmark development of the elder.

The challenges that come with Life may seem arbitrary and random, but they are the raw materials that form unique, powerful, and resilient human lives. Elders are not those who merely survived hardship; they know they are shaped by it, and they thrive because of it. Life has treated them roughly, and they are better off for it. As a result they have a different outlook on difficulty and a different capacity for dealing with it. They can feel confident about Life because it has put them to the test. They have a rare ability to respond that sets them apart.

Facing Responsibility

One of the things distinguishing an elder is responsibility. Responsibility expands throughout a lifetime, and in rare individuals reaches the point where it includes others in a way it never did before. This sense of responsibility goes deeper than the norm. Whereas a conventional person might feel some kind of outside force is responsible, and an autonomous person might take responsibility for him or herself, the elder is responsible to a larger body. Unlike others, elders consider and take responsibility for the groups they feel part of. This can include the human race and Life itself.

Responsibility is a daunting thing. Assuming it is hard. Accomplishing an expanded sense of responsibility requires that one learn how to take and give up control. This is not a lesson that is intuitively obvious. Elders shine here because they have been subjected to the challenges of Life. Difficulty, which they had no control over, has taught them that the only thing they do have any control over is themselves. This autonomous trait translates into an awareness that they need to exercise their ability to respond. Elders go further; however, they have taken this lesson to the group level. They know that the challenges of Life coax out of us, as individuals and as groups, the ability to respond. They personally increase a group's ability to respond by changing themselves.

Ruts, Old Horses and Addictions

It is easy to fall down on the developmental job. The cost is dear but isn't always obvious. The easy way is often preferable. Short-term gain trumps long-term growth. The price is right, so one often gives up other chances. It seems like a good trade-off at the time, usually bringing relief, but the consequences generally mean that development slows or stops entirely.

Sometimes it is our success that ensures that we stop growing. Old strategies that have saved our bacon or have given us advantages often prove to be, given enough time, the traps that prevent growth. Humans are creatures of habit. We are not above doing the same old repetitive thing that once worked. Like a rat in a maze, it is very human to seek rewards we know. The habitual becomes a yoke that ties us to the past. We create and live in ruts of our own devising. This normal human trait, however, has big implications. Aging doesn't stop. The future doesn't hold still.

The old, tired horse that carries us to the parade will not carry us beyond. This is a real pain in the ass. To go further we have to go beyond ourselves. This means abandoning all of the success strategies that have carried us this far. Becoming a beginner, a new being unshielded by what one has learned, is not easy or desirable. Choosing to begin again, to walk naked into the glare of the light, doesn't come easily. It is amazing some people do it. Life can be insistent; some are admittedly dragged into growth. But the benefits of hardship, with a feeling of something compelling stirring inside, impel some to ripen.

Elders have extraordinary experiences of transcending themselves. They go beyond the ruts, old ways, and attachments that have previously defined them. They have the experience, not always voluntary, of having given up control. They know that death awaits them, and that it can take many forms. For them, going back is one. They live, not for their own sakes, and they know it. This sets them apart and can make them obvious to the rest of us. All we need do to perceive them is grow ourselves.

Elders take awhile to ripen. They live by broader laws, but unlike the merely old, they lean towards the timeless. To the rest of us they may seem spacey and inattentive. But, sensitivity to deep time, to an expanded moment, is a part of what makes them so precious. Sometimes lacking short-term memory, the elderly, particularly elders, remember and remind us all of what is important — the whole sweep of Creation.

Why Do Some People Grow Beyond Merely Being Old?

Growing old, as I've shown, is organic. It is built into us, but we have some ability to regulate how much we grow. Not everybody is willing to submit to all that growth asks. The choice is only partly ours. This is an interesting aspect of being human. Humans grow because they have to. Growth is programmed into them. But they can influence the trajectory of that growth through their desire. Not every species has this capacity, and what we do with it is up to us. We are an extremely adaptable species, with enormous potential. The challenge we face, individually and as a species, is matching our growth and development with our historical circumstances. Elders are very adept at this.

While we are living, we are subject to the influences of our environment. In the earliest stages of life others are very influential. Later on, it is primarily our desire, our willingness, which determines what we make of what Life presents us with. In each case growth is a kind of dance. We are always partnered up with Life. Our steps determine the quality of our dance, but Life as our partner leads. Life leads. How we follow is totally idiosyncratic, unique, and up to us. The dance proceeds according to a combination of moves between the two. This is the privilege of being human, the contribution we humans make to creation, but it is always coupled with the ministrations of Life.

Human existence is tricky. Growing, which happens to us anyway, leads us into all kinds of tangled situations. The lament that new parents often express, that "there is no manual," is actually true for the whole of human life. All of us are confronted with the difficult task of determining for ourselves how much we are willing to use the adaptive capacities given to each of us. This is a matter of choice. And, it is always a challenge, for the choice has implications that go way beyond the moment. Life is involved in the dance too, and may be trying to forward evolution. The farthest reaches of human growth occur because of three factors, all of them involving the dance between Life and our choice. Elders are adept at all three of these factors.

Desire

Some of us are born with a fire in our bellies. There is a desire to be all that we can be. The military recognizes this, which is why this particular recruiting slogan resonates like it does. The fire of desire goes a lot deeper though. If family and cultural abuse don't bank the fire, then it blazes up into a search for true expression. Then all of us have a new aspect of creation to deal with. The Universe has expressed its need for diversity. And, through the fire of desire, growth is expedited. Uniqueness finds a form. And, if it goes far enough, it prompts the whole into changing. Desire is personal, expressed through the life of the individual, and it is more than that. It is an expression of the whole evolving.

Human life forms carry this particular burden/gift. It is part of the uniqueness of our species. We burn with the desire of the whole without knowing it. We live in a cultural time that doesn't recognize much of this — our human potential. So, we are doomed to do our best, to fight our way back upstream, never knowing if we will make it. Returning to the source, being all we can be, forwards the profuse diversity of Life. But the wildfire of wholeness, the expansion of the Universe, requires us to be more. Our lives fuel this fire.

Life Circumstance

The particular predicament that Life faces us with, the dance steps we are led into, form the raw materials of a life. We aren't in control of the hand we are dealt. John Lennon once sang, "Life is what happens to you when you are making other plans." It is true, but what's left out is that the quality of one's life is determined by how one responds, the moves one makes after Life's lead. Elders have learned how to follow. They show us all, if we are willing to notice, how much creativity can be involved in following, in responding.

Life can be harsh. It can also be also be incredibly kind. Both, in their way, present challenges, dance steps that coax out of us a response that creatively reveals and makes us unique. We have little choice but to become ourselves. The process of becoming isn't always fun. As the dance that Life puts us through proceeds, we pass through many possible selves. Some are alluring and comfortable and some are not. Becoming authentic is hard. Finding the signature response to Life, that is uniquely one's own takes a little time. One has to dance for a while to gain experience, to weather the frenetic movements of Life, to know oneself enough to determine a consistently self-expressive response. Elders know, via experience, how to dance.

Evolution

There is an inescapable storm-surge that runs through all of our lives. Change is ubiquitous; it is always happening. Our best-laid plans, the well-ordered lives we imagine for ourselves, the world we thought we lived in, all morph into something else. Our grip is slippery. Life twists and turns, and we are whiplashed around. Change seems to happen for its own sake. In fact, this is true. Evolution is shaking things up. It is looking for a new combination which will allow it to complexify, to become more functional and even more greatly creative. In the meantime, we get buffeted around.

Elders, however, have the winds of evolution behind them. They have adjusted to the restless and ever-changing nature of Life. They are distinguishable from the merely old because they have not become rigid. They know how to dance amidst transition. They are not caughtup in keeping pace; they have made friends with change by expecting it, celebrating it, and leaning into it. Elders have gained access to the wisdom of the ages because Life has had its way with them. They are evolution at work, and they hold out to us the possibility of knowing our own potential.

Becoming an Elder

Becoming an elder is not simply done. No amount of intention will deliver one to such a complex awareness. The journey to elderhood is made purely at Life's discretion. One's life is no longer solely one's own.

There are broader laws to adhere to, community to be responsible for, and a relationship with the larger mystery to maintain. All of this is an extension of human capacity. But the way there isn't rational or even logical. One is selected. Criteria are always changing. Becoming an elder isn't up to us alone; it is a product of collaboration with Life.

All one can do is position oneself to be selected. Until now this has been a kind of random process, at least on the human side. Elders show us, however, another possibility. The big picture, a larger reality, comes into view in the latter stages of life.

Occupying this world as fully as possible (and bringing along one's community) is what an elder's life is all about. But this larger reality has a vote. It determines who is fully ripe. Evolution proceeds by its own reason. Elders trust this apparent randomness as an expression of Life's wisdom.

The Differences

There are essential, organic differences between those who are merely old and those who have been made elders. They both are grey and wrinkled, they both suffer from ageism, and because they are treated the same, elders are made even more invisible. This has some very dramatic consequences for both old and young alike. Without knowing that other steps in development take place and are seen and valued, many of the old give up and never actualize their potential. The young suffer a deep loneliness and are disheartened by never knowing their own possibilities.

The upshot of all this is that old people by-and-large have access to the kind of experiential wisdom I refer to as known wisdom, but unless they have matured further and become elders, they tend not to have access to wisdom of the unknown sort. This is an important difference, one that has implications for the experience of wisdom. The wisdom of the past keeps us locked in the past, whereas the future resides in unknown terrain. If as a species we are doomed to live out the past, then known wisdom will suffice. If, however, we as a species hope to create novel and innovative responses to future issues, then unknown wisdom is essential.

Being mindful of which is which, knowing the two exist and how they differ, means several things become possible. The old are treated better. The past is more appropriately revered. Elders become visible. And, perhaps most importantly, the future becomes more familiar. Currently the unknown is treated more like the threatening stranger at the door. Instead, elders can transform the unknown into an unfamiliar neighbor. It is easier to open the door to a neighbor, unfamiliar though he or she may be, than to open it to a stranger. Knowledge is wisdom of a sort, but the wisdom of not knowing is something else — the future knocking.

Known Wisdom

The past is very reassuring; after all, it is what delivered us here. Staying true to it means staying true to what allowed us to survive. One cannot deny how compelling that is. Known wisdom is composed of what we know about how we got here and what we surmise about the future, based upon what we have experienced from the past. Seemingly, it increases our chances of surviving into the future. And, often, it does.

The stories from the olden times are thrilling because they offer us sure proof that there is a way out of the woods. It is hard to live without such assurances. The old seem to hold the keys to a kind of knowledge that is tested and proven. This form of wisdom is the hard-earned legacy of our species' journey. Without it we are doomed to go in circles, to recreate the wheel and stay forever in the dark ages. Known wisdom lets us steer through our species' long journey with a sense of control. This is important because the journey from prehistoric animal to modern human being seems relatively clean and sensible. It is a good story.

And, it is an essential one. Known wisdom is the key to our treasury. Without it, we know we cannot survive. Humanity could not exist and be what we are if we didn't have some kind of knowledge of where we have been and stories of our past adventures. Known wisdom gives us a sense of identity; it lets us distinguish ourselves; it provides us with a sense of our own fate. It is the way we make sense of our species' journey.

But, just like the ruts and routines of the past, the once wonderful successes that delivered us to a sense of competency, known wisdom can provide us with deep traps that hobble our thinking. The past — known wisdom — offers us so much, but at the same time corrals us and dims our imagination. Survival sometimes depends upon going beyond ourselves, going beyond the prevailing wisdom of the past.

Then known wisdom can get in the way. It can show something of the way, but it cannot deliver. The old are great repositories of the old ways, the traditions that have served, the milestones that prove that a journey is being made, but unless they have learned to live with the unknown, as some elders have, they are unreliable midwives of the future. Known wisdom, so wisely composed of what is past, is the knowledge that sometimes fails us when the future is ready to unfold. Then something more risky and uncertain is called for, something elders have been brewed up by.

Unknown Wisdom

The life of an elder is uncertain. It is precarious — not in a bad way, like always going over the edge — but more like always living at the edge, knowing deeply that crumbling earthquakes are happening. By learning to live with the unknown, the changing nature of Life, elders are acclimated to changing conditions. They are softened up — some would say stripped of all pretense. They live with an elegant capacity to recognize what is, including the unknown.

This form of knowing is rich with paradox. It is, after all, a form of unknowing. Paradoxical awareness, such as that found in *The Tao Te Ching* (The Way of Life), is a hallmark of elder awareness. As Lao Tzu says, things are not what they seem. The knowledge and wisdom of the past is not always the best way to address the future. Elders, because they themselves are products of the unknown, are able to see farther into the darkness because they are not looking for the familiar. They know that new forms emerge in unusual ways. They know how little they know. By virtue of their unknowing they are prepared to meet the unknown.

Unknown wisdom is also essential. It heralds new conditions, altered directions, a changing climate, curves and bumps in the road. Survival sometimes means change, not just to previous conditions but rather to new, completely unknown ones. The unforeseen becomes the new normal. The unpredicted becomes the new way. The human species has been blessed with an amazing capacity for adaptation. In fact, one could consider us adaptive marvels because we can embrace novelty.

Embracing the new isn't child's play, however. It involves a wise use of our consciousness, something the eldest and most developed of us do daily as a matter of survival. Elders surprisingly have the innocent wisdom of youth combined with the wily perspective of age, and therefore not only change more readily but more adeptly. Elders are used to, in fact, have learned to count on, surprises. They court the unknown, as a form of relationship with the death they know is coming for them. For that reason they are better suited to meet the kind of death that lives in the unknown.

Another attribute of unknown wisdom, in fact a new development in the perception of wisdom, is its collective nature. Wisdom sometimes is so complex and new that it takes many minds and modes of perception to become palpable. The truly new overwhelms individuals, sending them into paroxysms of self-doubt. A collective, a community of learners, is more likely not only to perceive novelty but to embrace it.

Collective wisdom comes about because people are able to see more of reality together than separately. This takes a different kind of relationship skills. This more thorough perception of wisdom is only accessible to those who have a capacity for appreciation of the advantages of differing. By appreciating the uniqueness of individuals and their idiosyncratic viewpoints and learning how to inquire into these differences, the nuances of a moment and its wisdom become available. Generally, this complex wisdom is more available to those who have acquired the relationship maturity that it takes to be really interested in the other's perception and perspectives. Elders are the ones most likely to have this maturity.

In other words, there is a social dimension to some forms of wisdom. In our rush to industrialized society, we have forgotten that there were not only wise people, but wise groups. This form of wisdom is not lost, but it is marginalized. It resides on the periphery where those who are generally held as society's outcasts live. The elderly, including elders, are treated this way, therefore what they are capable of seeing is largely neglected. Collective wisdom, by falling into the perceptual hole of Western society (where assumptions of disconnection prevail), is often missed, as is the form of maturity capable of it.

Conclusion

Elders hold several important keys. They have within them Life's capabilities. Wisdom would suggest that it is time that these capacities be released and more widely shared. Interestingly, to be believed in these capacities have to be experienced firsthand. This is another reason why elder community is so important. By and large, older people themselves don't really know their own capabilities. They need each other to find out and to believe themselves capable. There is no substitute for this direct experience. Wisdom of all sorts becomes most available when old people gather. The emergence of elders from such a gathering ensures that such wisdom is handled wisely.

The assumption that wisdom is only a thing of the past is one of the dangerous assumptions that haunts our efforts to act sustainably. Known wisdom, the wisdom of the past, is important and life sustaining, but insufficient when meeting the future. Unknown wisdom resides there. It takes the kind of openness that has been learned by elders to really meet and greet the unknown as it unfolds. Life has prepared some of us for such an occasion. Now our challenge is to empower each other for such moments.

RESOURCES

Age is not all decay.
It is the ripening, the swelling, of the fresh life within
that withers and bursts the husk.

— George MacDonald

Readings

A Bibliography for Elders-in-Training

The Making of an Elder Culture: Reflections on the Future of America's Most Audacious Generation, Theodore Roszak; New Society Press, 2009
    (Power of the Boomer generation and its future)

Audacious Aging, Edited by Stephanie Marohn; Elite Books, 2009
    (43 short essays on evolving through the passage of eldership)

60 On Up: The Truth about Aging in America, Lillian B. Rubin, Ph.D.; Beacon Press, 2007
    (Dispelling New Age myths and getting real about it)

In the Ever After, Allan B. Chinen M.D.; Chiron Books, 1989
    (A cross-cultural collection of elder fairytales)

What Are Old People For? How Elders Will Save the World
William H. Thomas, M.D.; VanderWyk & Burnham, 2007
    (Structure of an elder community)

Second Wind: Navigating the Passage to a Slower, Deeper, and More Connected Life, Dr. (William H.) Bill Thomas; Simon & Schuster, 2014
    (Same author as previous entry, on the shaping of this generation of older folks)

Age-ing to Sage-ing: A Profound New Vision of Growing Older, Zalman Schachter-Shalomé and Ronald S. Miller; Warner Books, 1995
    (More interior — spiritual eldering)

Eternity Soup: The Quest to End Aging, Greg Critser; Harmony Books, 2010

The Second Half of Life: Opening the Eight Gates of Wisdom, Angeles Arrien; Sounds True, Inc., 2005
    (Very beautiful book with practical and wise suggestions)

Ripening Time: Inside Stories of Aging with Grace , Sherry Ruth Anderson; Changemaker Books, 2013
    (A book about inquiry and discovery)

The Gift Of Years: Growing Older Gracefully, Joan Chittister; Bluebridge Books, 2008

The Creative Age: Awakening Human Potential in the Second Half of Life, Gene D. Cohen, M.D., Ph.D.; Harper-Collins, 2003

The Mature Mind: The Positive Power of the Aging Brain, Gene D. Cohen, M.D., Ph.D.; Basic Books, 2005

Keep Going: The Art of Perseverance, Joseph P. Marshall III; Sterling Publishing Co., 2006

Aging as a Spiritual Practice, Les Richmond; Gotham Books, 2012

Contemplative Aging: A Way of Being in Later Life, Edmund Sherman; Gordian Knot Books, 2010

The Art of Aging, Sherman B. Nuland; Random House, 2007

Your Second Life, Gay Luce; Delacorte Press, 1979

Fruitful Aging: Finding the Gold in the Golden Years, Tom Pinkson, Ph.D.; self-published, 2013

Celebrate 100: Centenarians Secrets to Success in Business and Life, Steve Franklin Ph.D. & Lynn Peters Adler, J.D.; Wily & Sons Inc., 2013

Centenarians: The Bonus Years, Lynn Peters Adler, J.D.; Health Press, 1995

Other Recommended Books

The Transition Handbook, From Oil Dependency to Local Resilience, Rob Hopkins; Chelsea Green Publishing, 2008
(Organizing and looking at the future)

Embracing Life: Toward a Psychology of Interdependence, David "Lucky" Goff, Ph.D.; Mill City Press, 2013
(Outlines the reality of relationship and connection)

Navigating the Coming Chaos, Caroline Baker; Iuniverse, 2012

The Hope, A Guide to Sacred Activism, Andrew Harvey; Hay House, 2009
(Discovering and practicing "sacred activism")

Useful Links

1. To read earlier articles about the Elder Salon, go to <www.elderssalon. blogspot.com>.

2. To hear and learn more about our radio program, *Growing an Elder Culture,* go to <www.elderculture.com>.

3. To read excerpts of *Embracing Life: Toward a Psychology of Interdependence* or to order it, go to <http://www.davidgoff.net>.

৵

NOTE: This story of Lucky's was written for use in some of the Elder Salon's monthly meetings, and is referenced in the Sample Agendas for March and April, 2012, p. 74.

A Dilemma Story for Our Time

—Lucky

Once upon a time there was a person who was born into this unbelievable world at this incredible time. He, or she, found that the challenge of being alive — during this difficult and unbelievable age — grew as time passed. The complexity of this time assured increasing change. As one of the people of this age, he or she wonders, it seems as if we all are confronted by an awesome tangle of conditions.

This world is grieving. The land is aching; so is the sky. There is no place or group of people to which one can go. Community consolation is hard to find. There is no hiding. The people have lost their trust for one another. The future looms like a stranger at the door.

There is great uncertainty in the air. All of the ways, even the old ones, are bridges failing under the weight of collective doubt. The cool, fresh, healing waters are becoming more precious as chemicals, climate change, and population pressure push them. A stiffness and formality covers things. Life is retreating. Footprints and trash are everywhere.

There are beacons of light, shining forth, lending the world a kind of mysterious and precious glow. There is hope, it resides in the recesses, and seems to have a life at the periphery, in the backwaters. But there is a terrible groaning that seems to be coming from all directions. The wild is dying off. Some kind of pervasive despair blankets the globe.

There are a few with more than enough and there are many more with not enough. This has always been so, but it has never been so out of balance. Humankind has yet to find a way to deal with such inequality. And it is growing.

The people are angry, grieving and confused. Fuses are short. We are caught in some kind of twisted fear. We know who is responsible. We want to hold them accountable. But we can't escape from awareness that we ourselves are culpable.

Denial is also rampant. There seems to be a positive patina that coats everything like a demented tide. The hurting goes on and on. It is met with stony silence. Hopelessness infects the taste and nutrition of our food, as unexpressed grief eats at us.

Life has lost some of its mystery. And on and on go the mechanical recitations of the ideological masses.

There is a sense of expectation rising — sometimes it envisions apocalypse, ruin, and demise and sometimes scenarios of a hoped-for transition (where a blazing future comes into sight). It seems that the wise talk is mystifyingly about both. 2012, Y2K, the End of the World, the Harmonic Convergence, the Rapture — they all keep returning in new guises. And always there is great uncertainty. Sustainability — of Life, of the future, of childish innocence, of the longing for completion, of the actualization of potential, of the struggle to love, of the human experiment — is in doubt.

This might be too great a question to ask, but the times seem to be calling for it. So, the dilemma is — given this world, and this time of uncertainty — *what is the form of consciousness that best serves the times?*

A Note about Transition and Elders

— Lucky

Transition Sebastopol serves to build a positive future by cultivating community resilience and responding to the great challenges of our times with inspired local action.

—Mission Statement, Transition Sebastopol

Now

We exist at an historical time, an evolutionary moment, where the future teeters uncertainly. Anxiety about Nature and survival has always faced our ancestors. Now it is our own form of nature that threatens. Clearly this is a complex moment. How will we respond?

We are the greatest threat we have yet to face. Our success is now our greatest danger. This is a time of a natural rite of passage. No one knows how to thread the eye of this dilemma. It seems reasonable to believe that the moment calls for creative attention, learning, and cooperation. By emphasizing community resilience the Transition movement offers a way through this dilemma.

To succeed, this movement needs combined effort. The future seems to be calling for us to become communal again, to rely once more upon our social nature. Our creative strength lies in our shared hearts. Transition offers us an opportunity to learn what we already know; our best chance for survival comes from fitting in, learning how to blend our perceptions and abilities, and enjoying together the lessons and gifts of nature.

Community resilience calls for community. Community thrives when human hearts are meaningfully connected. This is a strength of older people, especially those who believe themselves to be elders. The symmetry between Transition's emphases upon surviving into the future, along with the elders' focus upon living fully in the moment, is too great to ignore. Transition and elders can empower each other.

What Can Elders Offer Transition?

Old people are far more capable than has been assumed. They have, thanks to new longevity, the time and the energy that could drive a movement. Elders tend to be more capable of the kinds of relationships that optimize community. They are natural leaders, having benefitted from surviving hardships and losses, They have gained a lifetime of perspective and are particularly talented at seeing the big picture. It is in their natural developmental interest to give their abilities for the well-being of their community. And there will be many seeking a way to use their life energy well.

If Transition can make elders visible, then it could provide a way toward elder fulfillment. By practicing community which the elderly tend to be more capable of, transitional values can merge with a desire for meaning, caring, and learning. Elders will not only volunteer for change, but they will ensure that "doughnut holes" don't appear because, for them, it won't be volunteering but living fully. They have the most experience with surviving, thus offering us a real chance at sustaining the human experiment.

What Can Transition Offer Elders?

The symmetry between Transition's efforts and the needs of the old is striking. Elders thrive on meaningful service. Transition could harness the affections and energy of older people by supporting their communal awakening, by recognizing and valuing them, and by putting their enormous creativity, heart, and experience to work. Transition offers an opportunity to utilize their life energy well. A dramatic and alternative synergy is possible.

Transition merely has to do some genuine outreach. There are elders currently who would be glad to have a meaningful way to invest themselves. Millions more are on their way. Globally, they comprise what could be a great evolutionary force. If the Transition movement can respect what Nature has cooked up in its grey form, then the wisdom that comes with age can assist the needed changes.

Conclusion

We are at an unprecedented time in our species' life. It is apparent we need to develop a more mature set of capabilities. Elders already embody many of these needed characteristics. Our species' future, maybe the future of Life as we know it, may well depend upon how we respond to this moment. Nature has ripened some for such an occasion. Let's find a way to honor and utilize this resource.

To discover more about the Transition Movement in the U.S. go to <transitionus.org>.

Acknowledgements

— Lucky

I have been blessed by three things, which have motivated me to give words to the phenomenon of elders' community. The first is the many old people who have touched me in ways that have helped awaken me to the miracle we can be for each other. The second is the relationship of friendship and love between my partner Alexandra and me. Throughout growing the Salon, and now this work, I have been heartened and encouraged by the living example of a caring love. Finally, the Great Mystery has led me into many places, some of them very dark, but has always educated and fed me. The holding I'm receiving is being passed along. Thanks to all, and may you all find your heart's desire.

— Alexandra

I must give Lucky all the credit for this Handbook being anything more than a kind of nuts-and-bolts listing of what we learned as we created the Elders Salon rather than this much deeper and, I expect, more valuable piece about the abundant wonders and surprises possible while growing into elderhood. He is much more of a writer than I, and he has grown into a philosopher before my very eyes. It was, in fact, sharing pieces of his then-unpublished manuscript for *Embracing Life: Toward a Psychology of Interdependence* that captured me.

Additionally, the members of our Salon and its satellite activities are the true heroes and heroines of our discoveries. In particular we owe a debt of gratitude to the six elders who serve on our Guidance Council: Sandra Scotchler, Trymon Hunter, Dianne Monroe, Jeff Rooney, Gor Yaswen, and Bertha Jean Schmidt as well as to our KOWS Radio co-host, Donald True.

About the Authors

David "Lucky" Goff, Ph.D., M.F.T.

David served as adjunct faculty at the Institute of Transpersonal Psychology, where he employed large group processes to promote community and personal development. David also assists organizations, including therapeutic and spiritual communities, in their quests to create and sustain genuine community. His research into the "psychological sense of community" is the first to examine and describe the conditions that facilitate collective consciousness.

In 2003 David had a brain aneurism. As a result of his stroke, and the onset of a rare brain syndrome, he nearly died and ended up permanently disabled. This experience had a transformational effect on David, which made him "Lucky," and cued him into how radically connected all things are. This broader awareness now informs his approach toward what it means to be human.

He maintains a psychotherapy practice specializing in psycho-spiritual development. He also writes extensively about a psychology of interdependence (see *Embracing Life: Toward A Psychology Of Interdependence*), community, elders and the conditions that lead to a social and ecological sense of connection. He can be reached at <dg1140@sonic.net>.

Alexandra Hart

Alexandra was born in 1939 and has, therefore, had time to do many different kinds of things, though she identifies chiefly as a fiber artist, designer, and writer-editor. Pertinent to this work, she was editor of the Association for Humanistic Psychology *Perspective Magazine* for several years, designed books, and is still involved in many community-building activities as facilitator and participant. These include women's groups, mixed gender councils, and cohousing development in addition to many Transition Sebastopol Elders Salon activities.

Under the name of Alexandra Jacopetti or Alexandra Jacopetti Hart, she wrote *Native Funk & Flash: An Emerging Folk Art,* originally published by Scrimshaw Press, 1974, and recently reprinted in a third edition. It can be found on Amazon or Barnes & Noble or checked out at <nativefunkandflash.com> or <facebook.com/NativeFunkFlash>. Her work in this area is collected and shown by museums as evocative of those times.

Another aspect of her fiberarts career is expressed as a co-founder of the clothing pattern company Folkwear Patterns, begun in 1974. The remaining major area of her artwork is as a tapestry weaver. Large-scale tapestries hang in many homes and in corporate settings. Her macramé playground was the subject of an NEA-funded movie "The Saga of Macramé Park" filmed by Ben Van Meter. She can be reached at <ahart@sonic.net>.